THE EDUCATIONAL LEADER'S INTERNSHIP

MEETING NEW STANDARDS

P. LENA MORGAN, ED.D.
ALBERT S. GIBBS, PH.D.
C. JAY HERTZOG, ED.D.
VIRGINIA WYLIE, PH.D.
VALDOSTA STATE UNIVERSITY

TECHNOMIC
PUBLISHING CO., INC.
LANCASTER · BASEL

The Educational Leader's Internship
a **TECHNOMIC**®publication

Published in the Western Hemisphere by
Technomic Publishing Company, Inc.
851 New Holland Avenue, Box 3535
Lancaster, Pennsylvania 17604 U.S.A.

Distributed in the Rest of the World by
Technomic Publishing AG
Missionsstrasse 44
CH-4055 Basel, Switzerland

Printed in the United States of America
10 9 8 7 6 5 4 3 2 1

Main entry under title:
    The Educational Leader's Internship: Meeting New Standards

A Technomic Publishing Company book
Bibliography: p. 225

Library of Congress Catalog Card No. 96-60522
ISBN No. 1-56676-444-0

HOW TO ORDER THIS BOOK
BY PHONE: 800-233-9936 or 717-291-5609, 8AM–5PM Eastern Time
BY FAX: 717-295-4538
BY MAIL: Order Department
Technomic Publishing Company, Inc.
851 New Holland Avenue, Box 3535
Lancaster, PA 17604, U.S.A.
BY CREDIT CARD: American Express, VISA, MasterCard
BY WWW SITE: http://www.techpub.com

PERMISSION TO PHOTOCOPY–POLICY STATEMENT
Authorization to photocopy items for internal or personal use, or the internal or personal use of
specific clients, is granted by Technomic Publishing Co., Inc. provided that the base fee of US $3.00
per copy, plus US $ .25 per page is paid directly to Copyright Clearance Center, 222 Rosewood
Drive, Danvers, MA 01923, USA. For those organizations that have been granted a photocopy
license by CCC, a separate system of payment has been arranged. The fee code for users of the
Transactional Reporting Service is 1-56676/97 $5.00 + $ .25.

SECTION III: PERFORMANCE ASSESSMENT

PREFACE

This manual is intended to serve as a guide for students enrolled in an internship program in Educational Leadership, their field supervisors, school systems accepting interns, and university supervisors. It should not be considered as a comprehensive statement on the internship program. There most certainly will be aspects on which all parties will have to confer.

Purposes of the Manual

1. To address the needs of the educational leadership community by providing a structure upon which to build a field experience for the leadership intern program. Included within this structure are the following components:

    a. an overview of the internship program from its inception. Included in this is the conceptual framework of an educational leadership program and its component parts;

    b. an examination of the National Council of Accreditation for Teacher Education Guidelines for the Internship (1995) and the guidelines for the National Policy Board for Educational Administration (1993);

    c. The roles and responsibilities of the administrative intern program including those of the intern, the university, and the school in which the internship will be carried out;

    d. an outline of seminars which are designed address issues not covered in the intern's coursework, e.g., professional image, the need for ethics in administration, and a look at the three settings of administration (elementary, middle, and high school); and

    e. an examination of the various forms of intern assessment. This includes activities designed to synthesize the intern's coursework as it relates to the intern experience through coursework and in-basket activities.

2. To provide those involved in the educational leadership intern program, a format for development of the leadership portfolio.

3. To provide a quantitative and qualitative mechanism for evaluation of the leadership intern through the use of intern logs, the development of the intern's school development project, and the completion of field supervisor's evaluation form.

The authors would like to thank the following individuals for their contributions to this manual:

Richard Campbell, Lowndes County School System, Valdosta, GA

Melissa Fisher, Brooks County School System, Quitman, GA

Mary Ann Gibbs, Tift County School System, Tifton, GA

Kathy Keown, Thomasville City School System, Thomasville, GA

George Kornegay, Thomas County School System, Thomasville, GA

Wanda Sumner, Valdosta State University, Valdosta, GA

SECTION I:

KNOWLEDGE BASE

The purpose of this section is to review historical changes which have occurred in internship programs, examine the nature of the internship in educational leadership, and provide a model which demonstrates the role of the internship in educational leadership preparation programs of today. In addition, the 12 guidelines adopted by NCATE in October 1995, which provide the foundation for the internship, are presented. Corresponding knowledge and skill base as well as performance standards, adapted from the National Policy Board for Educational Administration manual, are given.

CHAPTER 1

TRENDS IN THE ADMINISTRATIVE INTERNSHIP

I. Introduction: The Problem

Today's leadership preparation programs face mandates for change as a result of national, state and local policies that demand institutional reform and accountability. Accreditation agencies and other professional bodies support these demands with their own guidelines. The America 2000 Goals (McKernan, 1994) sum up a growing consensus that school improvement must take place to serve the needs of all the nation's youth and contribute to a better world.

It is the school leaders in local schools across the country who must implement the changes necessary to meet these worthy goals for the future. In turn, universities bear responsibility for providing excellent leadership preparation programs that will assist school leaders in performing their increasingly demanding role. Inevitably, all components of leadership preparation programs are under scrutiny and have been under attack in the latest wave of ongoing educational reform (Griffiths, Stout, & Forsyth, 1988b).

In particular, the administrative internship has been a focus of public attention and concern in reform efforts (Peper, 1988). The internship has become a target of criticism for two reasons. First, for its lack of direct control from the university; and secondly, because of the various local/state expectations and requirements, the quality of the intern's administrative experiences differs from one location to another. In many instances criticism of the internship has been justified. These concerns should be the point of departure for the review of leadership preparation programs, strengthening them and exploring methods to make the internship the relevant culminating experience it should and can be for our future school leaders.

II. Historical Perspective

How the administrative internship came into being and developed through the years into an established component of leadership preparation programs clarifies the problems now faced and also directs educational leaders toward solutions to the problem. It must be remembered that before 1900 formal preparation programs for school administrators rarely existed. Schools were managed by teachers, teachers of teachers, teaching principals and others who learned on the job. They were hired by local communities as much for their moral character as for any skills they might possess (Campbell, 1987).

Reacting to demands for better prepared school managers to meet the needs of a growing society, the twentieth century ushered in the beginning of the Prescriptive Era in educational administration (Murphy, 1993b). Practitioners had been criticized for their lack of grounding in the management principles of the corporate world such as those proposed by Frederick Taylor (Hanson, 1991; Hoy & Miskel, 1991). In response, states began to require formal coursework for administrative positions and to certify graduates of preparation programs for employment. More and more principals and superintendents began their careers with a background of college training.

However, early training for administrators was essentially the same as that for teachers, and included an assortment of education courses and, inevitably, field study. Thus, the first administrative internships modeled that of the student teaching experience in teacher education, and both were originally similar in concept to the old craft apprenticeship (Campbell, 1987).

Trends in the administrative internship since the early days have paralleled trends in the development of leadership preparation programs in general. Beginning around 1910, the scientific management movement followed by the human relations movement of the 1930s and 1940s, particularly as these movements influenced the corporate world, led to changes in administrative preparation programs that persisted into the 1950s (Murphy, 1993b). The primary objective of the new programs was to differentiate training programs for school administrators from that of teachers. This objective was to be accomplished by helping students better understand the specific tasks and responsibilities that comprised the job of administration and to train them to perform successfully in the management roles they would assume.

Course content for administrators continued to be highly technical in nature throughout the Prescriptive Era, gradually incorporating the new emphasis on human relations in cooperative educational activities. These program components, as part of this new training, became the basis for the traditional administrative internship. The original purpose of the internship was to apply content, presumably taught and learned in the classroom, to a field experience jointly supervised by college-based faculty and senior practitioners. Application usually consisted of observing and participating in how-to activities. Weaknesses in the traditional internship were soon apparent not only in the typical loose supervision provided but also, more importantly, because of the nature of the program content itself. Coursework tended to be fragmented and disjointed, and professors paid almost no attention to the conceptual framework of the work of school administrators.

The scholarship of the Prescriptive Era has been described by Griffiths (1988a), Murphy (1993b) and others as naked empiricism and an encyclopedia of facts resulting in the development of fuzzy concepts that lacked the unifying power of interpretive theories. Typically, a professor of educational administration was a former school superintendent whose course content consisted of personal anecdotes or war stories, folklore and testimonials, and preachments about ways in which administrators should perform. Participants exited administrative preparation programs with little more than a do as I did philosophy.

Calls for improvements brought forth changes in college and university preparation programs. At mid-century the Prescriptive Era in educational administration gave way to a new Scientific Era that lasted well into the 1980s (Murphy, 1993b). Prescriptions drawn from practice were soon overshadowed by theoretical material drawn from the social sciences. For example, bureaucratic, systems, social systems and other theories were studied along with leadership, decision-making and change models with an eye to strengthening the knowledge base of educational administration. Preparation programs emphasized research and theory building to describe and explain task areas and processes. In discussions of theory versus practice, practice was downgraded and denigrated as consisting merely of disjointed and untested principles.

By tradition, the administrative internship retained its place in preparation programs, but it was not considered a high-status experience or even always required. Many internships were seriously limited in scope and all too often either were structured artificially with a set of insignificant and trivial responsibilities or not structured at all with learning left to chance. New or already overloaded faculty members were the first to be assigned responsibility for these field experiences.

As late as the mid 1980s, the typical internship was often disparaged as an experience of mutual convenience, with little regard for course sequencing, field placement, or qualifications of either school or university supervisors. According to Richards and Fox (1990), the intern, usually a teacher with a full- or at best a part-time classroom assignment, agreed to devote planning and lunch periods and before-and-after school time to perform duties assigned by the principal. Most principals gratefully gave extra duties to anyone willing to do them. This was an accepted trade-off for the privilege of completing the internship requirement for university degrees and state certification.

The resulting internship experience invariably incorporated control duties such as bus, lunch, hall and playground supervision. Usually included were minor responsibilities such as ordering textbooks, monitoring tests, front desk duty, miscellaneous paperwork and other cast-off duties that the principal preferred to avoid. These activities may be a necessary part of the job, but interns limited to them were poorly prepared for their first administrative positions. In short, the effective internships initiated by unique educators in unique settings during this Scientific Era were overshadowed in most leadership preparation programs by the situational constraints if not outright indifference to typical internships. Battle-scarred school administrators beleaguered with the difficult issues reflecting a diverse, changing society were probably justified when they complained that their university programs did not prepared them for an administrative position.

III. National School Reform

The public voices the conviction that contemporary school administrators are responsible for the crises in education. These administrators are often seen as incapable or unwilling to solve the array of problems that plague schools of today--violence, lack of discipline, drug abuse, truancy, low standards, poor curriculum, lack of motivation, lack of respect, and discrimination--the problems that are most often cited (Elam, Rose & Gallup, 1994). Since universities are responsible for the preparation of school administrators, it follows that these institutions are blamed for inadequately preparing them. It is commonly believed that universities have neglected their mission to serve society by the lack of attention in their programs to the twin themes of equity, i. e., responsiveness to the needs of specific constituencies, and excellence, i. e., responsiveness to the general needs of the country (Bacharach, 1990).

In the 1980s, a wave of school criticism and call for reform has placed every facet of leadership preparation programs under serious scrutiny with all program components found wanting. Content was irrelevant; instruction was dull; performance standards were conspicuously absent. For the last decade faculties in departments of educational administration have been strongly encouraged to evaluate and improve their own programs, and warned that if they do not do so someone else will take over the job. Indeed, the someone else has already forced many changes to occur by way of centralized federal and state legislation based on recommendations from business-heavy committees. Mandated standards have been incorporated into most leadership preparation programs with varying results (Bacharach, 1990).

The press for leadership-preparation reform at the national and state levels has led us to seek models for guidance in our efforts to make university programs more relevant. Perhaps, the worst accusation that can be hurled at educational leadership departments is to say that their programs are irrelevant, that they do not prepare future school leaders for the difficult task which awaits them. However, before rushing into programmatic changes, it is imperative to determine if relevance can be found in the Prescriptive and Scientific Eras. Questions that need to be asked are: Must the past be discarded and begun anew to reform and restructure leadership programs?; and, What and why must it be changed?

IV. The Need for Change

America needs a citizenry who knows how to learn in an organized and disciplined fashion, using the best methodologies and technology available today. Individuals need to know how to think and solve problems--and they must be motivated to learn purposefully from school, books, teachers, each other, and from all other available resources and experiences. Ensuring that all children learn what they need to learn in today's society is a challenge that has never before faced educational institutions in our country.

It must be kept in mind that the ultimate goal of education is to prepare children for their future. Children are the future. The influence of leadership preparation programs has the potential for far-reaching effects on school programs throughout the nation. This influence should be the ultimate goal of these programs. The responsibility of leaders at all levels includes the notion of vision as defined by Bacharach (1990) as "the ability to question established and entrenched traditions in light of the big picture, as well as a clear sense of what that big picture is." It is in this realm that the need for change is revealed.

Schlechty (1990), in discussing schools for the 21st century, pointed out that important aspects of the big picture can be learned from changes that have occurred in society. For example, Toffler (1980) predicted that the rapidly developing Information and Communication Ages, the Electronic Era, and the concept of a Global Village would force radically changed schools. Others have focused on the grim political, economic and ideological conditions of the 1990s. These conditions affect the life prospects of a diverse school population and expose a widespread and compelling need for quality education (Tozer, Violas, & Senese, 1995).

As society becomes more technological and information-based, those who have knowledge and know how to use it will have the power to function successfully in the 21st century. In this sense, Schlechty (1990) called schools "knowledge-work organizations." Viewing schools in this sense implies a fundamental shift in the way the curriculum is conceived and organized. In effect, the curriculum becomes the raw material for the knowledge-work process. The richer and more diverse the material, the richer the knowledge-work products will be. When students participate actively in the knowledge-work process, they take knowledge and skills embedded in the curriculum and make it their own.

If the assumption that schools today have problems reflecting societal changes and demands is accepted, and that the traditional curriculum can only promote a widening disparity in learning opportunities for today's youth, the need for change is clear. Program improvement is needed, and this is as true for teacher and administrator training as it is for the public schools. The key to such improvement is effective leadership. At all levels, the role of educational leadership requires the collaboration and combined know-how of thoughtful, purposeful people.

Leadership preparation programs need a united effort where practicing administrators and university professors alike assume a professional stance. These individuals must recognize themselves as leaders of leaders, as developers of leaders, and as creators of conditions in which other leaders cope and thrive. Schlechty (1990) maintained that leaders in knowledge-work organizations manage by values and results. Such leaders express visions and assess results. His belief that "purpose shapes vision and vision shapes structure" becomes a recurring theme throughout the remainder of this work.

V. The Professional Era

The recent wave of criticism of school administrators and how they are trained has been far more devastating and comprehensive than that accompanying the Prescriptive and Scientific Eras (Hallinger & Murphy, 1991; Murphy, 1993a). In fact, according to the American Association of Colleges of Teacher Education, "School administrators risk becoming an anachronism if their preparation programs in schools, colleges, and departments of education do not respond to calls for change in preparing them for professional leadership functions" (1988). Such criticism led to what Murphy termed the Post-Scientific or Dialectic Era in school administration (1993b). This new era of turmoil was characterized by a growing sense of professionalism among the educational leadership community. For example, both the American Association of School

Administrators (AASA) and the National Council of Professors of Educational Administration (NCPEA) have advocated the movement toward a professional school model in training programs (AASA, 1982; Murphy, 1993a). Such responses suggested that the new era in school administration could well be termed the Professional Era (Milstein, 1993).

From this vantage point, The University Council for Educational Administration (UCEA), an organization consisting of more than 50 leading universities, conducted a major review of the criticisms and needs of leadership preparation programs. This led to the publication of Leaders for America's Schools (UCEA, 1987). In the summary of this work, UCEA cited the need for major changes and called for the reconceptualization of preparation programs. Following this, the National Commission on Excellence in Educational Administration developed a new vision of school-based change that suggested differences in the responsibilities of school leaders as opposed to school managers (Griffiths, Stout & Forsyth, 1988b).

These different responsibilities supported the necessity for quality performance in schools and quality preparation programs in universities. Ensuring such quality will take a collaborative and coordinated effort by school districts, state agencies, professional associations and others in addition to the university. The major premise of The National Association of Secondary School Principals (NASSP) Consortium for the Performance-Based Preparation of Principals was that only coordinated efforts to prepare and support school administrators at preservice, entry and succeeding career stages can provide quality control of leadership preparation programs (NASSP, 1992). The National Association of Elementary School Principals (NAESP) supported the notion that study after study had identified areas of knowledge, specific skills and values that consistently distinguished leaders of effective schools. Therefore, the reasonable assumption is that common purpose and collaboration among formal stakeholders in the teaching-learning process can structure programs to help principals develop these essential understandings, skills and values (NAESP, 1990).

While consensus about the weaknesses of current preparation programs and the need for change exists, there is less agreement about alternative models. Nevertheless, the most frequent recommendations include an emphasis on values and social context, the perception of leaders with vision and competence, use of technology and newer methodologies in classroom instruction, cooperation between schools and colleges, and recognition of the importance of craft knowledge. The legitimacy of field-based learning experiences where knowledge and skills can be applied and demonstrated has been overwhelmingly reaffirmed (Murphy, 1993a).

Such recommendations have led in turn to general agreement on the key components that should be part of restructured entry-level leadership preparation in order to assure and assess quality programs. These components have been summarized by NASSP and include: (1) generic knowledge and skills of school administration, (2) substantive content related to task areas and processes of administration, (3) identification of role-specific behaviors to be demonstrated in field settings, and (4) procedures for monitoring and assessing attainment and application of knowledge and skills (NASSP, 1992).

It appears that the emerging trend during the Professional Era is toward ensuring competence through application and demonstration. In <u>Performance-Based Preparation</u> competence was defined as follows:

> Competence can be measured only through an accumulation of evidence, over time, that an individual is able to apply knowledge and perform certain functions and skills in ways which are perceived positively by both the individual and his/her audiences. This conceptualization emphasizes reliability (an accumulation of evidence), validity (apply knowledge and perform skills), and legitimacy (in ways which are perceived as being positive (NASSP, 1985).

Competence thus has a contextual nature. Students must develop in their initial studies knowledge, skills and values that can then be verified through performance in a field setting. The NASSP definition of competence is an example of the viewpoint of educational leaders who advocate a field-based component in preparation programs.

The stage is now set for the implementation of a new and effective internship program based upon a continuously developing knowledge base with educational reform at its center. The Danforth Foundation decided to apply its resources to help universities develop training programs that were more responsive to school districts' leadership needs (Milstein, 1993). This decision led to the Danforth Programs for the Preparation of School Principals (DPPSP) which by 1992 included 22 universities. This organization initiated two studies. The first study consisted of a survey of participating universities to determine ongoing program change efforts while the second study consisted of the selection of five representative programs to serve as models. Model programs included key reform components and which had been developed at universities representing different regions of the country. Case studies were prepared and by this time have been disseminated to some 500 higher-education institutions that prepare educational administrators across the country (Milstein, 1993).

In conclusion, examining alternative models and adapting them to meet local needs and settings is the new thrust and greatest challenge of the Professional Era in educational administration. The Professional Era thus involves a decentralization process whereby reflective educators are complementing national goals and centralized mandates for reform by working together to re-create their own leadership preparation programs in their own institutions.

VI. A Model for Today

With the change of presidential leadership in 1992, the <u>America 2000</u> education goals were retained but given expanded interpretations and focus (McKernan, 1994). New state administrations rapidly moved the impetus for reform to the local and institutional level. State Departments of Education were reorganized to become more service oriented.

A Conceptual Framework Model, is presented in this Chapter, depicting the relationship of components in a straightforward manner, while in fact there is overlapping and reinforcement. The flow of action is dynamic and cyclic in nature as students complete one program, enter another, and seek jobs. The first component of the model titled "Entry" contains the admission and individual assessment modes that are handled jointly by the Graduate School and the Department of Educational Leadership. Once students have met admission criteria and are accepted into the program, they flow into the second component titled "Planning." Here advisors are assigned and individual advisement occurs that results in a planned Program of Study for each student.

The third component titled "Coursework" contains the modes of knowledge, skills and application that serve as bases for all academic courses under the aegis of leadership (EDL), foundations (EDF), research (EDR), and psychology (PSY). This coursework includes six of the seven required leadership courses as well as core courses and electives. The seventh required leadership course, the administrative internship, is shown alone indicating the importance field study plays in the M.Ed. program.

"Evaluation," the fourth component, contains the vehicles used to assess the outcomes of completed M.Ed. degree and/or 5th-year certification programs of study. Exit assessments at this level include successful completion of 60 quarter hours of coursework for the M.Ed. degree and 35 quarter hours of coursework for 5th-year certification (the same leadership courses as required for the M.Ed. degree), passing a comprehensive examination and passing the State-administered Teacher Certification Test (TCT) in administration and supervision. The final component, "Follow-Up," includes recommendation for leadership certification, career guidance, assistance in job placement, and survey data collected from program graduates. "Follow-Up" is a combined responsibility of the department, College of Education, and various career placement and research services provided by the University.

The role of the EDL Advisory Council is denoted in the conceptual framework as a central body influencing all program components. This council meets as a group twice a year and is comprised of experienced administrators in the local service area who are interested in assisting with the continuing development of leadership preparation program. Taken as a whole, these administrators form a cadre of practitioners who can be called upon for information from the firing line and with whom cooperation can be established in school improvement projects. Feedback from this council is invaluable as a reality check in evaluating course content and methodologies against problems and needs graduates will face as they assume their own leadership positions.

VII. The Role of the Administrative Internship

The internship is the culminating experience at the Master's Degree level. This interpretation has implications that bear further exploration. Historically, many administrative internship programs have been a traditional course taken by students when convenient and loosely supervised by college faculty. In many cases, the course had been available but not required. Students who took it rated it as valuable but not particularly rigorous.

Regardless of various pronouncements, the internship has not generally been understood by either faculty or students to be a theory into practice experience where formal coursework was applied in a field setting. As university supervisors began to realize that a viable leadership preparation program should provide for this application process, program fragmentation had to be addressed. Questions which needed to be answered were: What was the knowledge base totality that our students were supposed to apply?; and What was the purpose of the internship? Decision-making would have to be shared by university supervisors, field supervisors and students. Those who have accepted the challenge of the revised internship have enjoyed a sense of involvement in which hard work was seen as a pay off.

As previously stated, "Purpose shapes vision and vision shapes structure" (Schlecty, 1990). The purpose is school improvement; the vision is leadership; and the structure is based on reason. To promote the teaching-learning process for the benefit of all children, it is the collaborative responsibility of the university, the field supervisors and the EDL advisory council to prepare school leaders by exposing them to the best available research and theory, to infuse them with a sense of professionalism and competence, and to help them understand how knowledge and skills can be applied with real people, problems and events.

VIII. Summary

In retrospect, it can be seen that the latest educational reform movement has involved strands of influence from the national, state and local levels, as well as from professional bodies and accreditation agencies. These influences serve as catalysts for change, however, only program by program change in institutions of higher education in collaboration with their constituencies can bring about valid change in leadership preparation programs. This change requires that individual faculties, working together with field-based professionals, face up to their reason for being and their purpose as professionals.   Vision and structure will evolve as reform is undertaken.

Historical trends can provide instructional background. The administrative internship has exemplified every era in the development of leadership preparation programs. Previously, the internship has been thoughtlessly accepted by convention, steeped in trivia, downgraded as the field of educational administration gained a semblance of respectability, and finally recognized as the valuable experience it should and can be. Each era is built upon the successes and failures of the one before, but it is our nature to grow onward and upward. If education is to gain credibility, the time to act is now.

DEPARTMENT OF EDUCATIONAL LEADERSHIP
CONCEPTUAL FRAMEWORK OF M.ED. PROGRAM

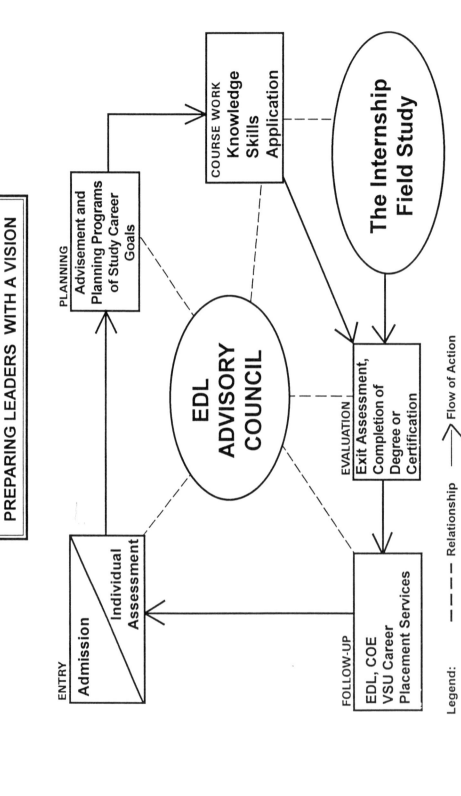

MOTTO
PREPARING LEADERS WITH A VISION

PLANNING
Advisement and Planning Programs of Study Career Goals

COURSE WORK
Knowledge Skills Application

The Internship Field Study

EDL ADVISORY COUNCIL

EVALUATION
Exit Assessment, Completion of Degree or Certification

ENTRY
Admission
Individual Assessment

FOLLOW-UP
EDL, COE VSU Career Placement Services

Legend: – – – Relationship   〉 Flow of Action

CHAPTER 2

EDUCATIONAL LEADERSHIP KNOWLEDGE AND SKILLS BASE

If principals are to meet the educational and developmental needs of their school, they must continually initiate action and respond to changing conditions. These initiatives and changes are often complex, ranging from the implementation of new local, state, and federal legislation to resolving explosive family conflicts. Technical skill or reliance on content knowledge alone is insufficient. The heart of professional practice lies between the two poles.

Given the changing nature of the school environment, it is impossible to prepare the future educational leaders for every situation which he or she may face. The purpose of this chapter is to help provide the administrative candidate with generalizable knowledge and skills to address new situations and traditional patterns. For example, key interpersonal skills like oral expression or motivating others, and core skills like problem analysis and data-based decision-making, assist a principal in solving unanticipated problems or in reversing negative developments.

Following a review of competency requirements of states within the nation, the National Council for the Accreditation of Teacher Education (NCATE) curriculum guidelines for advanced programs in educational leadership for principals superintendents, curriculum directors, and supervisors, adopted in October 1995, were selected as the foundation for this chapter. These guidelines were formulated through the efforts of the National Policy Board for Educational Administration (NPBEA) to 1) assist in the development of common and higher standards for the state licensure of principals; and, 2) develop a common set of guidelines for the NCATE accreditation of departments of educational leadership. These guidelines encompass 11 domains, through four broad areas, plus the process domain of the internship. Domains identified constitute the essential repertoire of knowledge and skills required of educational leaders for practice, which are not discrete from one another.

In addition to the NCATE guidelines, Knowledge and Skills, and Performance Standards have been adapted from the Principals for Our Changing Schools: Knowledge and Skill Base, which was developed by leaders in educational leadership working with the NPBEA. The strategy used to form the knowledge and skills base involved viewing the principalship from two perspectives: inductive and deductive. The outcome of these two processes constitutes the core of what educational leaders must know and be able to do professionally.

Adapted from the NCATE Approved Curriculum Guidelines with permission from NCATE
Adapted from the Principals for our Changing Schools with permission from NPBEA

AREA I. STRATEGIC LEADERSHIP

The knowledge, skills and attributes to identify contexts, develop with others vision and purpose, utilize information, frame problems, exercise leadership processes to achieve common goals, and act ethically for educational communities.

1. Professional and Ethical Leadership: Providing purpose and direction for individuals and groups; shaping school culture and values; facilitating the development of a shared strategic vision for the school; formulating goals and planning change efforts with staff and setting priorities for one's school in the context of community and district priorities and student and staff needs.

Guidelines

The institution's program prepares school leaders who understand and demonstrate the ability to:

1.1   Facilitate the development and implementation of a shared vision and strategic plan for the school or district that focuses on teaching and learning.

1.2   Understand and create conditions that motivate staff, students and families to achieve the school's vision.

1.3   Frame, analyze, and resolve problems using appropriate problem solving techniques and decision making skills.

1.4   Initiate, manage, and evaluate change process.

1.5   Identify and critique several theories of leadership and their application to various school environments.

1.6   Act with a reasoned understanding of major historical, philosophical, ethical, social and economic influences affecting education in a democratic society.

1.7   Manifest a professional code of ethics and values.

Knowledge and Skills

Strong leaders shape school culture and values, develop shared strategic visions, and formulate improvement efforts by performing specific tasks. They recognize and understand the behaviors that support and interfere with effective leadership.

A. Shaping school culture and values through:
* a well developed education philosophy;
* setting and communicating high expectations for students and staff;
* exhibiting an understanding of the school climate;
* facilitating shared understanding of culture and values;
* reflecting school culture in personal behavior;
* communicating values by participation in, initiating, and encouraging others to inaugurate celebration ceremonies and rituals;
* aligning reward systems with values;
* looking for evidence that the values of potential staff members meshes with those of the school; and
* awareness of effective and ineffective behaviors in shaping school culture and values.

B. Developing a shared strategic vision that through:
* future orientation;
* ownership of a personal sense of vision;
* tapping into the hopes and dreams of staff, parents, and students;
* facilitating the vision building process;
* conflict management; and
* maintaining support for the vision.

C. Formulating improvement efforts by:
* leading the school staff through a goal-setting process in which improvement areas are identified and actions for change are initiated;
* inviting staff members to initiate ideas for improving their school and educational programs;
* managing transition; and
* understanding that their school is composed of several interrelated systems, which are themselves part of a larger system (e.g., the school district or the community).

Performance Standards

To be competent in the professional and ethical leadership domain, effective leaders should be able to:

A. articulate a personal vision for their school and a well developed educational philosophy and set high standards for themselves and others;
B. gain insights into a school's culture and school members' personal hopes and dreams;
C. apply knowledge of socioeconomic and educational trends, innovations, and new paradigms to schools and assess how each might affect schools in the future;

D. influence and strengthen school culture by modeling core values, communicating values in symbolic ways, aligning reward systems with values, and selecting and socializing new members;

E. facilitate direction-setting processes within schools that require a high degree of member participation (e.g., assessing current school culture and values, building a school vision, developing organizational goals and strategies);

F. view their schools as a series of systems, as well as a system within a larger system (e.g., the school district or community);

G. foster innovation within their schools;

H. facilitate the development of school improvement efforts; and

I. utilize the leadership skills of staff and students to plan and implement the change process.

2. Information Management and Evaluation: Gathering data, facts, and impressions from a variety of sources about students, parent, staff members, administrators, and community members; seeking knowledge about policies, rules, laws, precedents, or practices; managing the data flow; classifying and organizing information for use in decision making and monitoring. Identifying and evaluating the important elements of a problem situation by analyzing relevant information; framing problems; identifying possible causes; seeking additional needed information; framing and reframing possible solutions; exhibiting conceptual flexibility; assisting others to form reasoned opinions about problems and issues. Determining what diagnostic information is needed about students, staff, and the school environment; examining the extent to which outcomes meet or exceed previously defined standards, goals, or priorities for individuals or groups; drawing inferences for program revisions; interpreting measurements or evaluations for others; relating programs to desired outcomes; developing equivalent measures of competence; designing accountability mechanisms.

Guidelines

The institution's program prepares school leaders who understand and demonstrate the ability to:

2.1   Conduct needs assessment by collecting information on the students; on staff and the school environment; on family and community values; expectations and priorities; and on national and global conditions affecting schools.

2.2   Use qualitative and quantitative data to inform decisions, to plan and assess school programs, to design accountability systems, to plan for school improvement, and to develop and conduct research.

2.3   Engage staff in an ongoing study of current best practices and relevant research and demographic data, and analyze their implications for school improvement.

2.4   Analyze and interpret educational data, issues, and trends for boards, committees, and other groups, outlining possible actions and their implications.

Knowledge and Skills

Information management. Before making decisions, administrators must identify the type of information they need and determine where and the most efficient way of obtaining that information. Educational leaders must collect, organize, analyze, and summarize their finding, and-when necessary and appropriate-share their findings with the others. More specifically, educational leaders must:

A. Determine what information is needed and why it is needed.
B. Select the appropriate sources for obtaining information.
C. Identify the appropriate strategies and/or tools for collecting information.
D. Collect information from a wide variety of sources.
E. Separate the information by element and develop a system for classifying and/or coding each.
F. Establish relationships or look for trends or patterns in information through qualitative and/or quantitative analysis.
G. Summarize and describe the information collected.
H. Present selected information in a logical and appropriate manner.

Evaluation. Educational leaders can become more effective problem analyzers/evaluators by understanding and practicing the behaviors associated with each component of the process model.

A. Recognition of a problem situation.
B. Gathering additional pertinent information from credible sources is crucial to problem analysis, and administrators should maintain their objectivity when collecting information.
C. Separation of relevant and irrelevant information and evaluation and integration of information to ensure that the problem is viewed from all perspectives.
D. While representing a problem, educational leaders should scrutinize it carefully and describe its causes and consequences.
E. Generating and testing hypotheses utilizing all available information.
F. Reanalysis of information and synthesis in problem redefining following hypotheses testing.
G. Administrators must be able to differentiate between sound and unsound assessments, if not they will be unable to plan, implement, or interpret a sound program.
H. The administrator must understand how all the assessments within a school fit together.

I. Administrators must know the issues involving unethical and inappropriate use of assessment information and ways to protect students and staff from misuses.

J. Instructional leaders must be able to assess the policies and regulations that contribute to the development and use of sound assessments at all levels.

K. They must assist the staff with setting goals for integrating assessment into instruction and assisting teachers in achieving these goals.

L. Effective instructional leaders evaluate teachers' classroom assessment competencies and they build such evaluations into the supervision process.

M. They are involved in the planning and presenting to staff developmental experiences that contribute to the development and use of sound assessment at all levels of decision making.

N. Instructional leaders use assessment results for building-level instructional improvement.

O. Instructional managers accurately analyze, interpret, and act upon building-level assessment information.

P. They create conditions for the appropriate use of achievement information.

Q. Educational leaders communicate effectively with school community members about assessment results and their relationship to instruction.

Performance Standards

After completing this domain, school leaders should be able to:

A. understand information collection as an ongoing process and recognize its importance;

B. perceive the interrelatedness between the information collection process and the other dimensions of professional practice;

C. diagnose the information collection needs of their schools;

D. identify various information sources, various strategies for collecting information, and the relative strengths and weaknesses of each;

E. collect information through multiple modalities;

F. use technologies as well as manual methods to organize and analyze school-based information;

G. summarize and describe information and present it in written and oral form.

H. identify problem analysis as a critical step in solving problems and as an integral part of their jobs;

I. analyze work problems in a systematic and logical manner;

J. categorize problems according to general type;

K. describe the relationship of problem formulation to problem solution;

L. illustrate the barriers presented by personal behaviors and situational factors to problem analysis;

M. describe useful steps for identifying and analyzing information related to problems;

N.   define connections between hypothesizing and problem analysis;

O.   describe the relationship of information synthesis to problem solution.

P.   reach logical conclusions, while making high quality, timely decisions based on the best available information; exhibiting tactical adaptability; and giving priority to significant issues.

Q.   describe the major components of an assessment program designed to evaluate student outcomes;

R.   explain the relationship of assessment to strengthening curriculum and instruction;

S.   identify the major role expectations for principals in providing for assessment programs;

T.   examine the data relationships between school goals and student outcomes;

U.   draw inferences for revising school programs based on assessment data;

V.   design accountability mechanisms based on assessment information;

W.   describe the relationship of standards to purposes for evaluating student performance;

X.   explain the relationship of assessment to improving student outcomes;

Y.   identify assessment policies that contribute to the development of sound assessment practices;

Z.   develop with teachers an outcome-based, goal-oriented curriculum;

AA.   describe several specific competencies required of administrators in their role as leaders of the site-based assessment program, as managers, and as communicators;

BB.   explain the relationship of student assessment to school assessment;

CC.   evaluate the assessment competencies of teachers; and

DD.   explain the relationship of assessment at the school site to assessment policies and outcomes at the district, state, and national levels.

AREA II. INSTRUCTIONAL LEADERSHIP

The knowledge, skills and attributes to design with others appropriate curricula and instructional programs, to develop learner centered school cultures, to assess outcomes, to provide student personnel services, and to plan with faculty professional development activities aimed at improving instruction.

3. Curriculum, Instruction, Supervision, and the Learning Environment: Understanding major curriculum design models; interpreting school district curricula; initiating needs analyses; planning and implementing with staff a framework for instruction; aligning curriculum with anticipated outcomes; monitoring social and technological developments as they affect curriculum; adjusting content as needs and conditions change. Creating a school culture for learning; envisioning and enabling with others instructional and auxiliary programs for the improvement of teaching and learning; recognizing the developmental needs of students; ensuring appropriate instructional

methods; designing positive learning experiences; accommodating difference in cognition and achievement; mobilizing the participation of appropriate people or groups to develop these programs and to establish a positive learning environment.

Guidelines

The institution's program prepares school leaders who understand and demonstrate the ability to:

3.1   Create with teachers, parents and students a positive school culture that promotes learning.

3.2   Develop collaboratively a learning organization that supports instructional improvement, builds an appropriate curriculum, and incorporates best practice.

3.3   Base curricular decisions on research, applied theory, informed practice, the recommendations of learned societies, and state and federal policies and mandates.

3.4   Design curricula with consideration for philosophical, sociological, and historical foundations, democratic values, and the community's values, goals, social needs and changing conditions.

3.5   Align curricular goals and objectives with instructional goals and objectives and desired outcomes when developing scope, sequence, balance, etc.

3.6   Develop with others curriculum and instruction appropriated for varied teaching and learning styles and specific student needs based on gender, ethnicity, culture, social class and exceptionalities.

3.7   Utilize a variety of supervisory models to improve teaching and learning.

3.8   Use various staffing patterns, student grouping plans, class scheduling forms, school organizational structures, and facilities design processes, to support various teaching strategies and desired student outcomes.

3.9   Assess student progress using a variety of appropriate techniques.

Knowledge and Skills

Effective leaders are proficient in curriculum design, development, and implementation. Specific areas of proficiency include:

A. Curricular designs are a means to an end; they are the "form" that follows "function," or the desired outcome. Accordingly, principals must know various curricular design organizational models and those that are most appropriate for reaching specific curricular objectives. Sometimes, these objectives require that a multidisciplinary approach be taken. Curricular designs also must respond to and reflect various student grouping patterns.

B. It is important to possess knowledge of major ideas and controversies involving curriculum design to differentiate among trends, fads, long-term problems, and issues. The history of U.S. education suggests that these trends, fads, problems, and issues are cyclical.

C. Curriculum content has received major attention from various critics. As educational leaders listen to calls for curriculum improvement, they need to be aware of changes that are occurring in major subject disciplines. It is imperative that they understand the ideas and arguments that drive these changes and how they relate to their school's overall curriculum.

D. By learning how to integrate the formal, informal, and hidden curriculum, instructional leaders can shape instructional programs that together are more powerful than any one curriculum on its own. The informal curriculum consists of the norms and mores that affect student behavior beyond the planned program. Every school has a "hidden" curriculum, which consists of cultural values that are communicated unconsciously.

E. Educational leaders must know how to apply the various forms of curriculum mapping to the various subject areas and how to use mapping data to develop and improve instructional programs. Mapping is the process by which taught curriculum is assessed and the resulting data are used for improvement efforts.

F. Curriculum alignment is an old concept involving transfer theory and cuing. It enables leaders to align curriculum with textbooks and tests and, thereby, to maximize the effects of specific tests. They are also able to understand the ethical and conceptual issues involved in alignment so that unethical practices can be avoided.

G. Effective leaders know how to select, use, and interpret a variety of assessment tools. They are able to explain to teachers and parents data results and their implications for curriculum development.

H. An evaluation program dominated by various types of pupil tests requires that instructional leaders know how to engage in data disaggregation and portfolio assessment and how teachers can use these data to improve pupil performance. This is especially important because schools are the individual units of accountability.

I. Fundamental to framing a curriculum is needs assessment. Current models include perception, gap-based, and outcome-based. Educational leaders must understand the generic steps and problems associated with each in order to use them to construct and validate curriculum plans. Also important is a familiarity with the various techniques of needs assessment, including surveys, Q-sorts, and delphi.

J. Educational leaders should know how to be responsive to state mandates that require student achievement gains in selected curricular areas as measured by specific testing instruments. Accordingly, they should have a general knowledge of the critical components of quality control and how their behaviors on a day-to-day basis will make a difference in their schools' performance. In addition, they should be able to tighten or loosen quality control elements to attain learner objectives or to meet externally imposed mandates.

K. Educational leaders are called on to make judgments and recommendations about the kinds of documents that are, or would be, most effective in improving learning. Such documents are called work plans because they define, shape, and sequence classroom teaching, which affects student learning. Work plans can take a number of forms: guides, scope and sequence charts, pacing charts, lesson plans, checklists, teaching and learning objectives, and hierarchies of difficulty.

L. Educational leaders must be able to translate intentions into work. Accordingly, they must know practical planning strategies that involve staff, parents, and students. They must know how to develop user-friendly action plans that are supported by stakeholder groups and are technical enough to provide meaningful direction.

M. Documenting the results of change and innovation is one of the crucial skills of administration. Leaders must have a fundamental grounding in basic evaluation strategies, including curriculum auditing. They must also understand the conditions that enable some models to be more effective than others.

N. It is imperative for principals to be knowledgeable of research-validated practices in schools. Formal research studies provide the most reliable and consistent base on which to upgrade, expand, and enhance the quality of teaching and curriculum design. Thoughtful reflective practice also contributes insight. School administrators must know how to evaluate and apply research and reflective practice if they are to improve their instructional program.

O. Learning style relates to how a student learns and likes to learn, for each student has his or her personal learning style. Current research suggests that learning style can be defined by the following domains: perceptual/cognitive, affective, physiological, environmental. Instructional leaders must understand the meaning and importance of these domains and have a working knowledge of the dominant learning style models and instruments. They must also know the range of learning style characteristics contained in each model and how these characteristics are assessed by the models. In addition, instructional leaders must know the major elements of style-based instruction, particularly how cognitive style deficiencies can be remediated or augmented.

P. Instructional leaders must understand the instructional application of learning style. They must know how teachers are taught to remediate and augment student cognitive skills deficiencies. Instructional leaders also must understand and help teachers to design learning resources and flexible environments to support the education of students with average or better cognitive skills. In addition, they need to understand the relationship between basic cognitive skills and higher-order thinking skills and organize the school learning environment to enhance student growth along this skill continuum.

Q. Effective instructional leaders are able to identify how various forms of scheduling or organizational structures can incorporate different teaching strategies. They can relate various types of desired learner outcomes to scheduling and organizational practices and indicating which will be constrained or improved as a result. In addition, they select and implement a model schedule or structure for a hypothetical school when given an explicit philosophy, a basic curriculum design, and information about pupil learning styles and faculty preferences.

R. Effective instructional leaders demonstrate an understanding that a teaching model can be a learning model, serving as a guide for student and teacher alike. They are able to recognize the differences between the syntax and structure of various teaching approaches.

S. Being able to explain the emerging practice of authentic assessment and the relationship between criterion- and norm-referenced performance tests is a skills demonstrated by effective leaders. They possess an understanding of and are able to explain the development of tests, their basic assumptions and limitations, and the major problems facing their fair construction. .

T. Because supervisory methods must be differentiated, effective instructional leaders should demonstrate knowledge and skill in a variety of supervisory procedures, including traditional, clinical, and democratic. They are able to identify strategies that lead to the renewal of tenured teachers and their continued motivation to grow.

U. Educational leaders need to know how to develop, adapt, and use various teacher evaluation forms and practices to ensure curriculum continuity and delivery. They also need reliable classroom observations as a measure of instructional effectiveness. Effective leaders constructively critique any formative or summative evaluation report on a teacher and indicate three ways professional performance could be improved.

V. Effective leaders know how to design a school culture for learning and can relate various learning conditions, technologies, grouping modalities, and teaching techniques to desired student outcomes. They identify initiatives to build a school culture that focuses on achievement and recognition.

W. Instructional leaders must understand the role their facility plays in reinforcing specific types of human responses. Furthermore, they need to alleviate the impact of obsolete facilities on the learning process by modifying the physical plant to support priority programs and attain desired outcomes.

X. Critical pedagogy is a process by which a school's total instructional program is examined to determine its benefits. It asks "whose norms" are being taught and "whose culture" is being held up as the one to emulate. Effective leaders are aware of the ways schools mirror larger social relationships and reproduce them in school routines and rituals. They know that schooling is not a neutral activity, that it can perpetuate existing socioeconomic inequities by the "hidden curriculum" if that curriculum is left unattended.

Y. Effective educational leaders need to relate various staffing patterns to instructional practices and student grouping options and configure them for program effectiveness.

Z. Site-based management holds educational leaders accountable for the operation of school programs and the allocation of resources. These expanded responsibilities require that leaders have increased knowledge of fiscal management, including the ability to tie expenditures to program objectives and instructional practices.

Performance Standards

Interns completing this competency should be able to:

A.   identify the key attributes of skilled instructional leaders;

B.   describe the main differences between weak and effective instructional practices;

C.   identify the major sources and findings of research on instruction;

D.   know how to assist teachers in utilizing reflective practice;

E.   describe their responsibility with school staff to set instructional objectives, develop a data base, identify staff development needs, implement desired changes, and evaluate program effectiveness;

F.   describe the implications of learning style for instructional design and staff development;

G.   identify classroom strategies that respond to various student learning styles;

H.   describe the major forms of school scheduling and organizational structures and their relationship to programmatic effects and potential learner outcomes;

I.   conduct an exercise in school scheduling or organizational structure with real data;

J.   explain the relationships among instructional objectives, scheduling, and teaching strategies;

K.   identify several current teaching models;

L.   understand the principles of measurement and evaluation, including alternative approaches to evaluation and their application to various instructional settings;

M.   analyze test data, explain their implications to teachers and lay persons, and link them to school improvement programs;

N.   discuss a variety of supervisory techniques and describe their application to teachers in various stages of career development;

O.   describe various models of observation and identify ways to ensure their reliability;

P.   identify several elements of school culture that support teaching and learning;

Q.   relate various grouping practices and technological initiatives to desired student outcomes;

R.   outline a change process to improve student outcomes;

S.   analyze relationships between school plant and instructional programs and suggest steps to modify a traditional facility to improve the learning environment and faculty collegiality;

T.   apply critical pedagogy to three disparate socioeconomic settings;

U.   describe several staffing patterns and their relationship to various instructional practices;

V.   design a budget process with staff that reflects school priorities for the instructional program;

W.   describe the curriculum as being broader in scope than courses of study;

X.   identify major influences on the curriculum;

Y.   connect curriculum design to instructional objectives;

Z.   describe the major movements in American curriculum development, and the assumptions upon which they are based;

AA.   define the role of educational leaders in curriculum design;

BB.   define the role of educational leaders in curriculum implementation;

CC.   define the merits and deficiencies of quantitative and qualitative evaluation systems to evaluate curriculum outcomes;

DD.   define the relationships among curricula, school organization, and society;

EE.   identify and define the relationships among the written curriculum, the taught curriculum, and the tested curriculum;

FF.   describe procedures for improving quality control in implementing curricula;

GG.   relate curriculum design and delivery to curriculum management;

HH.   describe current trends/issues in several content fields;

II.   discuss several curriculum organizational models and the relative merits of each;

JJ.   identify several current curricular issues and their historical antecedents;

KK.   describe curriculum mapping and its uses;

LL.   define curriculum alignment and its relationship to curriculum development;

MM.   analyze several evaluation instruments and describe strengths and deficiencies;

NN.   interpret the selection and use of a variety of assessment tools;

OO.   describe how schools can use data disaggregation to improve pupil performance;

PP.   conduct the basic steps involved in needs assessment; and

QQ.   involve teachers in the design, development, and management of curriculum.

4. Professional Development: Working with faculty and staff to identify professional needs; planning, organizing, and facilitating programs that improve faculty and staff effectiveness and are consistent with institutional goals and needs; supervising individuals and groups; providing feedback on performance; arranging for remedial assistance; engaging faculty and others to plan and participate in recruitment and development activities; and initiating self-development.

Guidelines

The institution's program prepares school leaders who understand and demonstrate the ability to:

4.1   Work with faculty and other stakeholders to identify needs for professional development, to organize, facilitate, and evaluate professional development programs, to integrate district and school priorities, to build faculty as resource, and to ensure that professional development activities focus on improving student outcomes.

4.2   Apply adult learning strategies to professional development, focussing on authentic problems and tasks, and utilizing mentoring, coaching, conferencing and other techniques to ensure that new knowledge and skills are practiced in the workplace.

4.3   Apply effective job analysis procedures, supervisory techniques and performance appraisal for instructional and non-instructional staff.

4.4   Formulate and implement a self-development plan, endorsing the value of career-long growth, and utilizing a variety of resources for continuing professional development.

4.5   Identify and apply appropriate policies, criteria and processes for the recruitment, selection, induction, compensation and separation of personnel, with attention to issues of equity and diversity.

4.6   Negotiate and manage effectively collective bargaining or written agreements.

Knowledge and Skills

The managerial and leadership qualities of administrators, as defined in the functional, interpersonal, and contextual domains, are essential to the conduct of staff development activities. Educational leaders must work with individuals and groups to formulate goals and to initiate, direct, and follow through on tasks. They must motivate others and exhibit sensitivity when working with them, and they must pay attention to cultural and philosophical values. These skills and knowledge are incorporated in this competency through the framework of the developmental model:

A. Educational leaders must be aware of the external influences that affect their schools and staff. Likewise, they must be up-to-date on district policies and planning procedures to assure that their schools' needs are met and that resources are made available for staff development. An adequate on-site data base is required to help compile and track this information.

B. Staff development is the organized means to carry out school improvement. Just as staff development strongly influences a school's culture, so does school culture influence staff and student performance. Educational leaders help create and sustain a school's culture. Their leadership abilities and management skills are essential, therefore, to planning and implementing staff development activities and to communicating program expectations to participants. Educational leaders need to be up-to-date on staff development research and practice, especially as these relate to school culture. Leaders should be knowledgeable about adult learning and training programs designed to transfer new skills to practice.

C. Educational leaders must be knowledgeable of staff development research and successful applications for each function. To be effective, they should be skilled in planning procedures, group processes, information sharing, management training, and delegation.

D. Implementation refers to the conduct of activities needed to complete each phase of the staff development plan. Properly planned and organized, each activity has specified tasks and objectives, a set timeline, and assigned responsibilities. Some activities will be contingent upon the acquisition of resources; others may require that consultants be brought on-site to conduct workshops or to confer with work groups; still others may require that activities be coordinated with other school and/or district personnel. According to the literature, an administrator's visibility during inservice is key to success. So, too, is staff participation in the planning and performance of staff development activities, and the use of school personnel as instructors; whenever possible, they should be given leadership roles.

Performance Standards

After completing this competency, interns should be able to:

A. describe the essential characteristics of a staff development program and the four primary staff development functions;

B. analyze and critique descriptive accounts of successful programs in terms of planning, implementation, and evaluation, and determine if these programs incorporated all of the essential characteristics and primary functions of staff development;

C. demonstrate mentoring, coaching, and conferencing skills;

D. be knowledgeable of action research methods as they relate to the investigation and resolution of classroom and school problems;

E. discuss the relationship between staff development and the following: supervision, staff evaluations, the incorporation of new knowledge and skills in classroom practice, and program evaluation;

F. conduct literature searches for each of the items above and identify sources that will keep knowledge and skills up-to-date; and

G. review evaluation studies to identify questions investigated, methods used, principle findings, and the effects of staff development activities.

5. Student Personnel Services: Understanding and accommodating student growth and development; providing for student guidance, counseling, and auxiliary services; utilizing and coordinating community organizations; responding to family needs; enlisting the participation of appropriate people and groups to design and conduct these programs and to connect schooling with plans for adult life; planning for a comprehensive program of student activities.

Guidelines

The institution's program prepares school leaders who understand and demonstrate the ability to:

5.1   Apply the principles of student growth and development to the learning environment and the educational program.

5.2   Develop with the counseling and teaching staff a full program of student advisement, counseling, and guidance services.

5.3   Develop and administer policies that provide a safe school environment and promote student health and welfare.

5.4   Address student and family conditions affecting learning by collaborating with community agencies to integrate health, social, and other services for students.

5.5   Plan an manage activity programs to fulfill student developmental, social, cultural, athletic, leadership and scholastic needs; working with staff, students, families, and community.

Knowledge and Skills

Educational leaders must have an understanding of program goals and alternative procedures and structures for achieving those goals. In addition, because they chiefly act through others to implement and oversee programs, educational leaders must be skilled at working with diverse groups of professionals and community members. Finally, they must communicate to individuals and groups within and outside their schools that student guidance and development concerns are central to the total school program and must be integrated with instruction. Critical areas in which administrators must possess knowledge and skills include:

A. Student Growth and Development

- expecting and influencing others to expect performances for which students have readiness and ability;
- expecting and requiring others to expect variations in student readiness and ability, even when norms are used as general guidelines;
- challenging students with reasonable expectations;
- recognizing developmental roots in students' behavior; and
- recognizing the strength of youth group mores in mid-adolescence and working to strengthen their beneficial values.

B. Student Guidance and Counseling

- recognizing that counseling programs must have a solid rationale if they are to benefit the school's academic function;
- allowing the counseling staff to spend most of their time on duties central to individual counseling or group guidance;
- facilitating interprogram planning so that the work of counselors and teachers is complementary;
- working with the counseling staff to provide a complete array of services to students, their parents, and faculty;
- helping to establish priorities to prevent counselor overload at the expense of quality;
- reflecting and understanding of the basic principles of counseling when working with guidance personnel and faculty;
- arranging for information processes that recognize language and cultural diversity;
- knowing the availability of counseling resources within the school and community and arranging or encouraging their efficient use; and
- protecting the privacy rights of students by establishing appropriate procedures and effective supervision.

C. Student Activities

- using accurate position descriptions and selecting advisors who have appropriate interests and abilities;
- working with staff and a thorough analysis of student needs and interests to create a comprehensive activities program;
- working with staff and within district guidelines to manage an accounting system for all activity funds;
- working with others to provide appropriate recognition to students and faculty associated with student activities;
- offering leadership development activities to elect student officers; and

- providing information to all students about the student activities programs and encouraging their participation.

Performance Standards

Examples of adequate performance by educational leaders in providing leadership for student guidance and development programs are described for each of the three major areas of the competency.

A. Student Growth and Development
- Presented with a sample statement of student responsibilities and associated discipline system, the intern can analyze the document applying basic principles of human growth and development relevant to student age levels.
- Presented with part of a sample curriculum, the intern can critique the sample and/or suggest review questions based on basic principles of human growth and development.
- Presented with a situation involving a faculty member who lacks understanding of the basic principles of student growth and development, the intern can describe an appropriate staff development intervention.

B. Student Guidance and Counseling
- Given an inquiry from a teacher who wants to know why counselors do not have the same duty roster as teachers, the intern can use basic counseling principles and practices to explain what counselors do with their time.
- Given an inquiry from a counselor who wants to know why his/her presence is needed in the entry areas during student arrival times, the intern can use basic counseling principles to explain the need for the counselors visibility and interaction with students.
- Given a student who is having difficulties with his parents, the intern can outline supplement community resources.
- Given a school with attendance problems, the intern can draft a plan that involves counseling and instructional staff members and integrate classroom and guidance activities to address the problem.
- Presented with a challenge by the superintendent and the school board during budget approval processes, the intern can develop a cogent defense counseling and its costs.
- Faced with the need to find a counselor, the intern can develop a job description that outlines the qualifications and duties of the position.

C. Student Activities
- As an elementary school intern, is able to describe how school-wide student government can be integrated with instructional and management programs.

- As a middle school intern, is able to describe the variety of student activities that a typical student population would sponsor during school-time activity periods.
- As a high school intern, is able to develop a job description for a student activities director serving the needs of a racially diverse student population.
- Presented with a case involving the publication of racially sensitive material in the school newspaper, the intern can critique the case using principles of school law and a sample district and school policy.
- Can explain the relationships between student activities and instructional programs and can describe ways to monitor the comprehensive opportunities each provides.
- Can identify criteria by which student activities programs may be evaluated.

AREA III. ORGANIZATIONAL LEADERSHIP

The knowledge, skills and attributes to understand and improve the organization, implement operational plans, manage financial resources, and apply decentralized management processes and procedures.

6. Organizational Management: Planning and scheduling one's own and others' work so that resources are used appropriately, and short- and long-term priorities and goals are met; scheduling flows of activities; establishing procedures to regulate activities; monitoring projects to meet deadlines; empowering the process in appropriate places.

Guidelines

The institution's program prepares school leaders who understand and demonstrate the ability to:

6.1   Establish operational plans and processes to accomplish strategic goals, utilizing practical applications of organizational theories.

6.2   Apply a systems perspective, viewing schools as interactive internal systems operating within external environments.

6.3   Implement appropriate management techniques and group processes to define roles, assign functions, delegate effectively, and determine accountability for attaining goals.

6.4   Monitor and assess the progress of activities, making adjustments and formulating new actions steps as necessary.

Knowledge and Skills

Effective organizational oversight is a function of specific skill development, an individual's personality, and the individual's desire to expand his or her capabilities in this competency. Some individuals appear to be well organized, natural planners; their personal traits often carry over into their professional lives. Other individuals appear to be absent-minded, inefficient, and careless in their personal habits, yet have learned through self-discipline to apply the skills necessary for providing excellent organizational oversight. Leaders who have 'natural' organizational skills exhibit key thinking skills and usually apply interpersonal evaluation skills. Administrators who simply master the mechanics of a management technique usually are disappointed with the limited impact of their new skill on effective organizational oversight.

Effective organizational oversight has five stages:
- sets plans to accomplish goals;
- schedules and plans resources and activity flow;
- establishes procedures to regulate activities;
- empowers process at appropriate places; and
- evaluates impact of goals and operational procedures.

Performance Standards

To be considered competent in the organizational oversight competency, the intern should be able to:

A. work with faculty, parents, students, and other school stakeholders to translate a shared vision into a strategic plan;
B. work with school stakeholders to establish operational plans that support strategic goals;
C. define roles and relationships for implementing and monitoring strategies and operational plans;
D. identify available and needed resources to implement long- and short-range plans;
E. implement global oversight strategies to determine how organizational goals are affected by other goals;
F. initiate appropriate management techniques to implement long- and short-range plans;
G. work collegially with teachers, parents, and community to reorder the organization in fundamental ways to make it more responsive to its environment;
H. establish standing plans, policies, standard operating procedures, and rules and regulations that facilitate the implementation and monitoring of strategic and operational plans;
I. develop a pattern of participatory decision making, teamwork, and two-way communication that permeates every aspect and activity of the school organization;

J. build intrinsic rewards into the organization structure so that students, teachers, parents, and other stakeholders in the school operation are empowered by actions that appropriately support the goals of the school; and

K. lead school stakeholders in a holistic evaluation of strategic and operational goals, the resources that have been allocated to achieve those goals, the processes by which those goals have been pursued, and the impact that the pursuit of those goals has had on the organization and its stakeholders.

7. Interpersonal Relationships: These competencies recognize the significance of interpersonal connections in schools. They acknowledge the critical value of human relationships to the satisfaction of personal and professional goals, and to the achievement of organizational purpose. Acting with a reasoned understanding of the role of education in a democratic society and in accordance with accepted ethical standards; recognizing philosophical influences in education; reflecting and understanding of American cultural, including current social and economic issues related to education.

Guidelines

The institution's program prepares school leaders who understand and demonstrate the ability to:

7.1   Use appropriate interpersonal skills.

7.2   Use appropriate written, verbal, and nonverbal communication in a variety of situations.

7.3   Apply appropriate communications strategies.

7.4   Promote multi-cultural awareness, gender sensitivity, and racial and ethnic appreciation.

7.5   Apply counseling and mentoring skills, and utilize stress management and conflict management techniques.

Motivating Others: Creating conditions that enhance the staff's desire and willingness to focus energy on achieving educational excellence; planning and encouraging participation; facilitating teamwork and collegiality; treating staff as professionals; providing intellectual stimulation; supporting innovation; recognizing and rewarding effective performance; providing feedback, coaching, and guidance; providing needed resources; serving as a role model.

Knowledge and Skills

Effective leaders motivate their staffs to achieve personal, professional, and educational excellence. In doing so, they draw on the five clusters of knowledge and skills outlined below.

A. Educational leaders monitor the degree to which staff feel challenged by their work. They design positions that require a variety of challenges rather than highly repetitive tasks. The staff members are moved into positions or add job responsibilities that provide them with opportunities to learn new skills. Effective leaders design school schedules to allow time for teacher interactions. They encourage teachers to use this time for joint planning and problem solving and the sharing of teaching strategies. Educational leaders remind staff that their work contributes to an important end: the education of children. They articulate to staff the conviction that schools can have a major, positive impact on society.

B. Effective leaders involve staff in decisions about school policies, plans, and practices. They ask staff for their opinions, suggestions, and advice in meetings and in chance encounters. Educational leaders allow staff a fair amount of discretion in carrying out their daily activities. They encourage staff to exercise independent judgment and are not constantly looking over staff members' shoulders. Nevertheless, they realize that staff members vary in their readiness for autonomy; experience and competence make some members more willing or able to work independently. Effective leaders articulate to staff the importance of interacting and communicating with parents. They make time available for parent-teacher conferences and create events that bring parents and staff together.

C. Educational leaders provide performance feedback through informal interactions and formal evaluations. Their feedback is candid, timely, and specific. Effective leaders ensure that performance evaluation processes are in place in their schools. They work with staff to select and implement procedures that generate feedback, such as assessment centers or paper and pencil confidential feedback instruments.

D. Effective leaders articulate performance expectations with their staff. They communicate these expectations consistently and frequently and express confidence in the staff's ability to meet high work standards. They model performance expectations through their behaviors and actions. Educational leaders find ways to help staff members improve their work effectiveness. They have staff set work and self-development goals. They provide opportunities for formal education and training, as well as on-the-job coaching. Effective leaders encourage staff members to talk with them about obstacles they encounter.

E. Educational leaders are aware of what various staff members find rewarding: what their needs are, what they want to accomplish, which rewards they find important, which rewards reinforce good performance, and which rewards have little impact. They provide both tangible and intangible reward for effective performance. Effective leaders give personal praise and public recognition in appreciation for a job well done. They hold special events to honor student and staff achievement and offer symbolic rewards, such as trophies, buttons, or citations. They celebrate and express pride in the accomplishments of their schools.

Performance Standards

To demonstrate competence at motivating others, interns should:

A. provide staff with job challenges and intellectual stimulation;
B. encourage teamwork and collegiality among teachers;
C. articulate the positive impact staff are having on children;
D. practice participative decision making;
E. be aware of the amount of autonomy various staff members need;
F. encourage close teacher-parent relationships;
G. provide face-to-face and written performance feedback;
H. be aware of various types of feedback systems;
I. understand their impact as role models;
J. enhance individual productivity;
K. articulate performance expectations;
L. be aware of the rewards that staff members value; and
M. provide tangible and intangible rewards for good performance.

Interpersonal Sensitivity: Perceiving the needs and concerns of others; dealing tactfully with others; working with others in emotionally stressful situations or in conflict; managing continually stressful situations or in conflict; managing conflict; obtaining feedback; recognizing multicultural differences; relating to people of varying backgrounds.

Knowledge and Skills

It is not enough for an educational leader to "feel" sensitive. They must express sensitivity in their interactions if they are to build and maintain positive relationships. Two conditions are necessary if an administrator wishes to be known as a sensitive leader:

A. They must understand how personal factors affect his or her perceptions, feelings, and actions toward others and act accordingly. Effective leaders listen carefully and empathetically. They delay the formation of impressions about others until adequate information or observations are acquired. Understood is the critical importance of maintaining and enhancing the self-esteem of others. Educational leaders maintain emotional control and avoid stereotypes of sex, race, or ethnicity.
B. Effective leaders must behave in ways that promote a caring environment. To achieve this, they anticipate the emotional effects decisions and actions might have on

others. Responses are tactful and respectful in emotional situations. Educational leaders encourage feedback from school groups and respond immediately to their suggestions and recommendations. They encourage others to share information that is relevant to organizational goals. They recognize the importance of praising others and using a person's name when conversing with him. Effective leaders show respect and courtesy toward others. They help others save face when taking a different position.

Performance Standards

To demonstrate competence in interpersonal sensitivity, interns should:

A. exhibit behaviors that promote a more positive and caring interpersonal relations climate;
B. use observation skills effectively to gain information about others;
C. choose the physical setting for interactions and set a tone that reinforces sensitivity regardless of the nature of the meetings;
D. manage conflict by reducing emotions and increasing mutual respect;
E. solicit the perceptions and concerns of others, and seek information from others;
F. recognize achievements and professional contributions;
G. describe the process by which an individual predicts what will occur in a social interaction; and
H. illustrate the dynamic and interactive nature of sensitivity.

Oral and Nonverbal Expression: Making oral presentations that are clear and easy to understand; clarifying and restating questions, responding, reviewing, and summarizing for groups; utilizing appropriate communicative aids; being aware of cultural and gender-based norms; adapting for audiences.

Knowledge and Skills

While some people seem to have an innate ability to communicate, many others have acquired equally strong communication skills through study and practice. Oral and nonverbal communication requires skill, knowledge, and judgment regarding message content, transmission methods, and so forth. Educational leaders must understand these choices and make knowledgeable and skillful decisions about them. The following are suggestions for improving verbal and nonverbal communication and for giving appropriate feedback.

A. Verbal Communication
• To understand a message, effective leaders must first listen to it. Much knowledge can be gained through active listening, and with knowledge, appropriate feedback can be given.

- Educational leaders must deal honestly with all of their constituents. They should not be afraid to admit a lack of knowledge or understanding. They should express their ideas with passion, not with overloaded emotion, and should strive to express disagreement without being disagreeable. A positive image should be projected that is consistent and natural when it comes to intonation and word choice.
- Effective leaders should use appropriate grammar and vocabulary. They should be brief, yet specific, and avoid educational jargon.
- Educational leaders should present factual information in a simple and logical way, using specifics whenever possible to paint a more vivid picture.
- Effective leaders do not let problems fester. They take a positive stance when communicating new ideas and discuss them at length with all concerned before making decisions about implementation. The timing of a message can be just as important as its content.
- Educational leaders should facilitate communication flowing to and from their schools.
- Effective leaders deliberately think through available choices and choose the optimum setting for the type of message they want or need to send.
- Trying to see things from the audience's perspective and empathizing with the audience when appropriate is a characteristic of effective leadership. Educational leaders use language that is understandable and meaningful to the audience.
- Effective leaders plan and rehearse their presentations to assure that their messages will be received and that they do not waste other people's time.
- Educational leaders should carefully plan how they will transmit their messages, remembering that how a message is transmitted is just as important as what the message contains.

B. Feedback Skills
- Effective leaders maintain direct contact and not engage in side tracking behaviors such as shuffling papers, tapping fingers, writing notes, etc.
- To demonstrate that they are listening and understand the speaker, educational leaders restate or paraphrase the important parts of the speaker's message.
- Effective leaders encourage the reluctant to communicate by showing concern for their feelings.
- A probe is a comment or a nonverbal cue leaders can use to encourage individuals to continue talking about a particular subject.
- Effective leaders encourage individuals to find their own solutions before offering advice or solutions. Shared problem-solving efforts are helpful and create feelings of trust among individuals.
- Giving others an opportunity to express their thoughts and feelings is important, especially if they are irate, frustrated, or emotionally disturbed. Communications flow more easily between leaders and others when there is this "give and take"; the communications also become more satisfying.

C. Nonverbal Communication

- Actions often speak louder than words, and so do nonverbal messages. Educational leaders are sensitive to their nonverbal communication.
- Most people study other people's eyes when looking for social acceptance. People tend to look longer and more often at those they trust, respect, and care about.
- Voice and message must be congruent. Educational leaders should therefore strive for a tone that communicates friendliness and openness, even to strangers.
- In most human relationships, touching can give encouragement, express tenderness, and show emotional support. While a simple pat on the back for a job well done is a much used and usually an accepted form of praise by principals, gender differences complicate this form of communication. Educational leaders and teachers should discuss this matter to determine what is preferred by all parties concerned.
- People reveal what they feel about themselves and others through body posture and movements. Body orientation indicates status, as well as how much a speaker likes a listener. Accordingly, the more direct a leader's orientation, the more positive his or her attitude will be.
- Effective leaders should carefully plan group meetings with regard to physical space. They should choose the most appropriate setting, arrangement of furniture, and placement of guests. In addition, they should learn to "read" the space needs of others, including the need for "intimate" space, the 1 to 2 feet surrounding individuals that should not be entered until a personal rapport has been established.
- Whether intentionally or not, principals send messages by the way they are dressed and groomed (see Chapter 4).

Performance Standards

Oral and nonverbal expression. To demonstrate competence in oral and nonverbal expression, the intern should:

A. identify effective and ineffective non-written behaviors;
B. be sensitive to nonverbal communication behaviors in yourself and others;
C. choose appropriate channels, timing, and settings for intended communications;
D. articulate ideas and beliefs clearly, using proper grammar and word choice;
E. use positive listening skills;
F. send and receive feedback;
G. communicate equally well with teachers, students, parents, peers, district and state personnel, and community members;
H. be aware of cultural and gender factors in communication;
I. be skilled at giving effective presentations to large and small groups;
J. choose appropriate settings for meetings and make appropriate physical arrangements; and
K. use current media technology to enhance and improve communication.

<u>Written Expression.</u> To demonstrate competence in written expression, the intern should be able to:

A. express ideas clearly in writing;
B. write appropriately for different audiences such as students, teachers, and parents; and,
C. prepare brief memoranda, letters, reports, and other job-specific documents.

Knowledge and Skills

The wide variety of documents that educational leaders must prepare, together with the range of audiences with whom they must communicate, places some extraordinary demands on leaders to write clearly. It is essential, therefore, that effective leaders possess a level of writing skill sufficient for these expectations. This requires practice as well as knowledge, for writing is a craft improved primarily by practice. Specifically, educational leaders must be knowledgeable of:

A. the stages of the writing process (prewriting, drafting, revising, and editing);
B. the types of documents they will be called on to write and the circumstances under which they are written;
C. the standards for written materials must meet to assure coherence, precision, and accessibility; and
D. the group management skills required for working on collaborative projects.

Performance Standards

One of the primary goals for educational leaders is to communicate effectively through well written and well organized documents that are tailored to specific audiences. The performance objectives below are designed to meet this goal. To demonstrate competence in written expression, the intern should be able to:

A. understand the importance of strong writing skills to their careers and schools;
B. assess one's current writing skills and attitudes;
C. understand and apply the four-stage writing process to job-related documents;
D. identify various types of job-specific documents and the functions each serve;
E. produce a variety of well targeted documents that are structurally, grammatically, and technically correct;
F. work cooperatively with others to develop written materials;
G. give and receive feedback on writing skills; and
H. use computer technology to enhance and improve the professionalism of written communications.

8. Financial Management and Resource Allocation: Procuring, apportioning, monitoring, accounting for, and evaluating fiscal, human, material, and time resources to reach outcomes that reflect the needs and goals of the school site; planning and developing the budget process with appropriate staff.

Guidelines

The institution's programs prepares school leaders who understand and demonstrate the ability to:

8.1 Identify and analyze the major sources of fiscal and non-fiscal resources for schools and school districts.

8.2 Acquire and mange financial and material assets, and capital goods and services, allocating resources according to district or school priorities.

8.3 Develop an efficient budget planning process that is driven by district and school priorities and involves staff and community.

8.4 Perform budget management functions including financial planning, monitoring, cost control, expenditures accounting, and cash flow management.

Knowledge and Skills

The knowledge and skills necessary to assess needs and formulate goals are developed in Competencies 1, 2, and 4. After working with others to determine school needs and goals, educational leaders develop a plan to procure and apportion needed resources, manage them throughout the school term, and evaluate the outcomes of this apportionment. Information gathered throughout the year and included in the summary evaluation directs leaders in the definition of needs and goals and subsequent resource allocation.

A. Planning includes the procurement and apportionment of resources that will meet the goals and needs established for the time cycle. Resources are defined broadly and include not only dollars but the services and objects purchased with dollars. Educational leaders must be able to develop a budget that reflects staffing and facility requirements and the program needs that parent, student, and community members agree are relevant and appropriate. They must be knowledgeable about specific statutes and state and district regulations governing the budget process. Skills are also needed to assess staff and community desires, to develop marketing and public relation programs, to make computer projections, and to plan strategies for enhancing interpersonal relations.

B. Administrators who intend to procure fiscal, personnel, and material resources must possess knowledge of traditional and nontraditional funding sources. In addition, they should have skills in grant seeking and grant writing. Knowledge of district discretionary funding policies and community resource pools is also valuable.

C. Skill in the efficient yet equitable distribution of resources is important. Educational leaders must be knowledgeable of state laws, district regulations, and negotiated contract restrictions that govern the assignment and the use of resources. They also must understand the rationale for building contingency funds, have knowledge of costing concepts, and be skilled in involving subordinates with the decision-making process. In addition, in the wake of greater parent and student choice among schools and programs, leaders must be able to attract new clients, to match the strengths of teachers with the needs of students, and to establish activities that support curricular and co-curricular programs.

D. Managing resources includes accounting for, monitoring and reapportioning resources as necessary during the specified time cycle. Accounting for resources is more than fiscal accounting. It includes accountability for materials, equipment, and personnel assignments and performance. Administrators must be knowledgeable about state and district regulations governing fiscal accounting. The intent of monitoring is to affirm apportionments, guard against ineffective allocation, and intervene with appropriate resources when faced with unexpected challenges. The ability to assimilate information quickly, make decisions, and implement change is required to reapportion resources midcycle.

E. The purpose of evaluation is to collect highly objective data that indicate change in specified areas. Educational leaders need to know how to develop surveys that accurately assess attitude changes among students, staff, and parents; use academic progress data to ascertain if academic goals are being met; and determine the impact of secondary elements on the allocation cycle. They may consider employing the quantitative analyses used in the planning phase to evaluate the results of an implemented allocation.

Performance Standards

After completing this competency, interns should be able to:

A. design resource allocation systems;
B. describe the role of resource allocation in meeting school goals;
C. identify various nontraditional resources available to schools;
D. design a strategy to gain resources from non-district sources;
E. describe the relationship of resource procurement to resource appointment;
F. design a monitoring and reapportionment system for resource use;
G. develop an accountability system for resource use;
H. connect resource allocation to student outcomes;

I. develop a system for staff participation in determining goals, apportioning resources, and evaluating use of resources;

J. develop and administer a school budget and an activities budget;

K. define resources as human and material as well as fiscal;

L. employ technical procedures such as spreadsheets, planning charts, and program budgeting;

M. develop a school purchasing system; and

N. design and administer a materials and equipment inventory system.

9. Technology and Information Systems: To be technologically literate/competent, an educator should have comprehensive skills, knowledge, and understanding of educational technology to specifically include: audio visual equipment and peripherals, computer hardware, software, and peripherals, and educational, ethical, and social issues as they relate to educational technology.

Guidelines

The institutions's programs prepares school leaders who understand and demonstrate the ability to:

9.1   Use technology, telecommunications and information systems to enrich curriculum and instruction.

9.2   Apply and assess current technologies for school management and business procedures.

9.3   Develop and monitor long range plans for school and district technology and information systems, making informed decisions about computer hardware and software, and about staff development, keeping in mind to the impact of technologies on student outcomes and school operations.

Knowledge and Skills

The knowledge and skills necessary for the operation and use of audio visual (AV) and computer hardware include:

A. understand AV and computer hardware (their systems, network, peripherals, and their relationship to each other) and understand how both may be used as teaching-learning tools.

B. be able to apply software appropriate to the AV or computer platforms used.

C. monitor the rapid changes in technology in order to make educated decisions when necessary.

D. discriminate between technology as a tool and technology as a problem.

E. acknowledge people's "technology anxiety" and learn the means by which to overcome it or the alternatives to using technology.
F. monitor changes in educational issues as each relates to changes in technology.
F. understand legal and ethical aspects of copyright laws for printed and electronic material, including what constitutes computer crime.
G. understand social and ethical issues arising from the impact of media and computers on society and other such issues that will arise with the expansion of technology.
H. monitor changes in social issues as related to changes in technology.

Performance Standards

To demonstrate competence in technology and information systems, the educational leader should be able to:

A. apply skills in developing and implementing AV instructional materials;
B. use software for managing instructional programs and in school management;
C. select AV or CAI software for a specific educational purposes; and
D. demonstrate basic skills in using word processing, spreadsheet, database, graphics, and telecommunications.

AREA IV. POLITICAL AND COMMUNITY LEADERSHIP

These domains reflect the world of ideas and forces within which the school operates. Explored are the intellectual, ethical, cultural, economic, political, and governmental influences on schools, including traditional and emerging perspectives.

10. Public Relations: Developing common perceptions about school issues; interacting with internal and external publics; understanding and responding skillfully to the electronic and printed news media; initiating and reporting news through appropriate channels; managing school reputations; enlisting public participation and support; recognizing and providing for various markets.

Guidelines

10.1 Analyze community and district power structures, and identify major opinion leaders and their relationships to school goals and programs.

10.2 Articulate the district's or school's vision, mission and priorities to the community and media, and build community support for district or school priorities and programs.

10.3   Communicate effectively with various cultural, ethnic, racial, and special interest groups in the community.

10.4   Involve family and community in appropriate policy development, programs planning, and assessment processes.

10.5   Develop an effective and interactive staff communications plan and public relations program.

10.6   Utilize and respond effectively to electronic and printed news media.

Knowledge and Skills

Public relations is more than writing press releases that communicate a positive school image. It is more than producing newsletters that keep parents abreast of organizational goals and activities or creating programs that reward student and staff performance. Ultimately--as Patrick Jackson, former president of the Public Relations Society of America, has said--it centers on building relationships that change attitudes.

Educational leaders need to be able to change negative attitudes and build on positive ones to develop public support for education in general and schools in particular. This support must be earned with each day and school year, and public relations is the vehicle through which this occurs. As a systematic management function, public relations requires sensitivity and careful planning.

Administrators have no choice but to engage in public relations because, they are responsible for building and maintaining the reputations of their schools. If schools are to be viewed in a positive light, leaders must develop and implement effective programs. Because they lack the resources available in the private sector, it is crucial that their programs be low-cost, practical, and based on proven theory.

The two essential theories of public relations are the Four-Step Public Relations Process and the Diffusion Process. The Four-Step Process consists of research, planning, communicating, and evaluating. During the research stage, educational leaders identify key internal and external audiences, ascertain their level of knowledge, choose the most appropriate medium to reach them, and collect the information that will be communicated to them. During the planning stage, leaders set measurable objectives, establish time lines and resources, and assign responsibilities for implementing the planned activities. During the communication stage, they deliver their message via brochures, newsletters, meeting and through other appropriate media. Finally, during the evaluation stage, educational leaders determine whether or not their messages have been received and their objectives met. The Diffusion Process (Jackson, 1986; Cutlip, Center, & Bloom, 1985) allows administrators to communicate more than information; it enables them to change attitudes by identifying the five information-processing steps people take when making major decisions: awareness, interest, evaluation, trial, and adoption.

Performance Standards

To demonstrate competence in public relations, interns should:

A. construct public relations plans for their schools that illustrate knowledge of the Four-Step Public Relations Process and the Diffusion Process;
B. identify their schools' internal and external audiences and design specific messages for each;
C. use mass and interpersonal communications techniques to influence people's attitudes;
D. use one or more techniques to assess a targeted group's level of understanding about a community issue or belief;
E. identity strategies consistent with the mores of a targeted audience;
F. differentiate between understandable language and educational jargon;
G. define and implement programs in which all school staff are informed of school activities and have an opportunity to provide input;
H. identify the major opinion leaders within their communities;
I. understand how to initiate news coverage and respond to reporters' questions;
J. understand the special public relations needs that arise during crisis situations; and
K. evaluate communication technologies that would be useful to their schools.

11. Educational Law, Public Policy and Political Systems: Acting in accordance with federal and state constitutional provisions, statutory standards, and regulatory applications; working within local rules, procedures, and directives; recognizing standards of care involving civil and criminal liability for negligence and intentional torts; and administering contracts and financial accounts. Understanding schools as political systems; identifying relationships between public policy and education; recognizing policy issues; examining and affecting policies individually and through professional and public groups; relating policy initiatives to the welfare of students; addressing ethical issues.

Guidelines

The institution's program prepares school leaders who understand and demonstrate the ability to:

11.1   Apply knowledge of federal and state constitutional, statutory and regulatory provisions and judicial decisions governing education.

11.2   Apply knowledge of common law and contractual requirements and procedures in an educational setting.

11.3   Define and relate the general characteristics of internal and external political systems as they apply to school settings.

11.4   Describe the processes by which federal, state, district, and school-site policies are formulated, enacted, implemented and evaluated, and develop strategies for influencing policy development.

11.5   Make decisions based on the moral and ethical implications of policy options and political strategies.

11.6   Analyze the major philosophical tenets of contemporary intellectual movements and analyze their effect on school contexts.

11.7   Develop appropriate procedures and relationships for working with local governing boards.

Knowledge and Skills

This competency requires knowledge of principles that limit authority, define individual and corporate liability, and inform standards of educational and managerial practice. Competency for educational leaders in this area would reflect knowledge of:

A. federal constitutional provisions applicable to a public education system;
B. federal statutory standards and regulatory applications relevant to public schools;
C. state constitutional provisions, statutory standards, and regulatory applications related to public school operation in a selected state;
D. standards of care applicable to civil or criminal liability for negligent or intentional acts under a selected state's common law and school code; and
E. principles applicable to the administration of contracts, grants, and financial accounts in a public school setting.

To use policies and political influence effectively, educational leaders must possess knowledge and skills in the three areas below:

A. The power-solution dimension draws on the knowledge and skills acquired in the functional domains. It incorporates knowledge of key concepts drawn from the literature on policy analysis.
B. The power-relations dimension draws on the knowledge and skills acquired in the functional domains, interpersonal domains, and contextual domains. It incorporates knowledge about the concepts embraced by the framework and information on major actors at various levels of the system, their goals, resources, strategies, incentives for action, and their impact on education policy. This dimension also includes knowledge about interest group actors such as teacher associations,

business alliances, private foundations, and community "influencials," as well as networks that mobilize around various issues in curriculum, testing, finance, student life, etc. In addition, it encompasses knowledge of community power relationships and the micropolitics of schools.

C. The normative dimension draws heavily on the Strategic Leadership competencies. It incorporates knowledge of the broad social values that frame educational policy debates and related concepts associated with ethical interactions. It also requires moral and ethical reasoning skills.

Performance Standards

To demonstrate competency in legal and regulatory applications, the intern should be able to:

A. demonstrate knowledge of federal constitutional provisions that apply to the public education system by identifying judicially recognized individual right guaranteed by the First, Fourth, and Fourteenth Amendments to the U.S. Constitution;

B. Demonstrate knowledge of federal statutory and regulatory provisions that influence public education by identifying:
- judicially recognized interpretations of the purpose and intent of federal statutes and regulatory provisions prohibiting discrimination;
- educational procedures required under federal statutes and implementing regulations; and
- statutory and regulatory standards applicable to copyright infringement, access to public documents, and record keeping.

C. demonstrate knowledge of state constitutional, statutory, and regulatory provisions governing a state's educational system by identifying:
- the statutory powers and duties of elected officials, education boards, administrative officers, and school principals in a selected state;
- the standards and procedures of administrative law, public disclosure, and record keeping in a selected state;
- the statutory and regulatory criteria applicable to certification, selection, evaluation, corrective discipline, dismissal, nonrenewal, or reduction in force in a selected state; and
- standards and procedures applicable to provision for minimum competencies, compulsory school attendance, curriculum development, facilities maintenance and construction, and finance in a selected state.

D. demonstrate knowledge of the standard of care applicable to civil or criminal liability for negligent or intentional acts under a selected state's common law or school code by identifying:

- legislatively mandated or judicially recognized elements of liability for negligence in a selected state;
- legislatively mandated or judicially recognized elements of intentional tort liability in a selected state; and
- legislatively mandated elements of statutory liability in a selected state.

E. demonstrate knowledge of principles applicable to the administration of contracts, grants, and financial accounts in a school setting by identifying:

- statutory or regulatory powers and constraints related to the principals' power to contract for goods and services in a selected state;
- powers and duties applicable to the management and administration of the contract of employment; and
- legislatively or judicially defined constraints applicable to the management of grants and financial accounts.

To demonstrate competence in policy and political influences, the intern should:

A. articulate the general characteristics of political systems and the manner in which those major characteristics apply to school systems;

B. describe the formal relationship between federal, state, local district, and school-site policies;

C. identify the theories of action in an existing or proposed policy;

D. assess the means-end relationships embedded in policies in light of available evidence and develop conditional recommendations regarding the ability of policy options to attain their stated aims;

E. describe how an existing or proposed policy interacts with other policies and how it complements or challenges the norms and routines of the school;

F. describe how actors in various arenas are (or are not) able to acquire the relative power advantage on particular policy issues;

G. assess the conditions under which prominent political strategies are more or less likely to be effective;

H. develop if-then scenarios that outline alternative political strategies that could be employed to mobilize support for or resistance to particular policy proposals;

I. profile the power relationship in their local school setting and indicate how these power relationships affect the likelihood that particular proposals can be enacted and implemented;

J. articulate how policy options affect particular dimensions of quality, equity, efficiency, and liberty;

K. assess the political interests and ideals of relevant constituent groups inside and outside the school setting; and

L. define and defend the value premises and ethical principles that will guide and govern their behavior in political arenas.

AREA V. INTERNSHIP

The internship is defined as the process and product that result from the application in a workplace environment of the strategic, instructional, organizational and contextual leadership Guidelines. When coupled with integrating experiences through related clinics or cohort seminars, the outcome should be a powerful synthesis of knowledge and skills useful to practicing school leaders.

The internship includes a variety of substantial concurrent or capstone experiences in diverse settings planned and guided cooperatively by university and school district personnel for credit hours and conducted in schools and school districts over an extended period of time. The experiences should reflect increasing complexity and responsibility, and include some work in private, community, or social service organizations. An optimum internship would be a year-long, full time experience. Part time internships involving limited periods of time are insufficient.

Participating school districts would be committed to the value of internships and supportive of these Guidelines for the internship.

Guidelines

12. Internship: The internship provides significant opportunities in the workplace to synthesize and apply the knowledge, and to practice and develop the skills, identified in the eleven Guideline areas. Therefore, the preparation program:

12.1 Requires a variety of substantial in-school/district experiences over an extended period of time in diverse settings, planned cooperatively and supervised by university and school district personnel.

12.2 Establishes relationships with school leaders acting as trained mentors/clinical professors who guide individuals preparing for school leadership in appropriate in-school/district experiences.

12.3 Includes experiences in social service, private, and/or community organizations.

VI. Summary

An internship program in educational leadership should provide the intern with as many supervisory and administrative experiences as possible. The intern should be prepared to initiate action and respond to changing conditions within the school environment. Reliance on technical skill or content knowledge alone is insufficient.

SECTION II:

THE SCHOOL/UNIVERSITY CONNECTION

The purpose of this section is to make the connection between what takes place in the field and expertise supplied by the Educational Leadership faculty. With all the changes taking place in schools today, many interns become inundated with the day-to-day functioning of the school and their particular assignments within the internship. Through the visits of the university supervisors, the interns have the opportunity to interact with and gain insight from an individual who is not intimately connected to the school. In addition, the visits of the university supervisors provides the intern with a touchstone to discuss various aspects of the assignment, both from the university intern program and from the field-based requirements. Two key elements to this linking of the school and community are found in the area of Roles and Responsibilities of the Intern and the Saturday Seminar.

Chapter 3
Roles and Responsibilities

I. Internship--Nature and Value

The purpose of any internship program is to provide experiences capable of bringing insight to professional educators both entering and currently practicing in public schools. An internship involves field placement; a first hand work experience in which the student has an opportunity to learn how academic knowledge can be applied in the educational setting. In this situation the student becomes a participant-observer in the field under the direction of a field supervisor, while receiving academic credit from a university supervisor. The intern is subject to the authority, rules, and regulations of the sponsoring school district. It is hoped that through these experiences, perspective administrators may more clearly discern patterns in their administrative performance. The intern should be able to determine the effectiveness or ineffectiveness of actions performed or observed, with regard to administrative competence. Thus, the participant gains valuable work-related experience which will give him or her a competitive advantage when applying for a position after graduation.

II. Internship Requirements*

A. Before a student is approved for an internship, the following conditions must be met:

1. A "B" average or higher in Master's degree course work.

2. Graduation or Master's level certification requirements to be met at the conclusion of the internship quarter/semester.

B. As part of the application process, the student must sign the Student Agreement (see Appendix A).

C. If the application is approved, the student must establish contact with and be accepted by a school administrator. A statement of acceptance must be completed by the field supervisor (see Appendix A).

*The student's advisor must approve any deviation from these requirements.

III. Academic Credit

For academic credit, the internship program stipulates the following minimum requirements:

Administrative Activities

An average of fifteen (15) hours of administrative activities per week are required. These activities may include, but should not be limited to activities known as duties. Field supervisors should provide meaningful tasks and insure that activities reflect the entire scope of educational leadership.   A daily log of administrative activities and observations keyed to the principal competencies must be kept by the intern (see Appendix B). In addition to daily comments, this log should contain a weekly reflection of activities and observations.

Policy and Governance

Interns are required to attend at least one school board work session and one school board meeting during the quarter/semester of their internship. A written reflection of the meeting should be attached to the agenda.

Comparison of Administrative Styles

The administrative intern is required to shadow an administrator in a school or school district other than the one in which he/she is employed. This shadowing experience should be written in 15 minute intervals, and contain a reflective observation, and be included in the intern's reflective journal.

School Improvement Project

A school improvement mini-project incorporating a minimum of 6 of the NCATE Principal Competencies (see Chapter 2). This project must receive the approval of both the field and university supervisors (see Appendix C).   One formal presentation of this project is required for completion of the internship. (*Note-Public School Standards, School of Excellence, handbooks, or accreditation paper work will **not** meet this requirement.)

Community Service Involvement

Each administrative intern is required to become an active participant in a social service, private and/or community organization. Because of the teaching assignments of some interns, selective participation will be expected as well as providing assistance at organization functions.

Leadership Portfolio

Information on this requirement is found in Chapter 5.

Saturday Seminars

Attendance at Saturday Seminars is required of all interns. Further discussion of this topic is covered in Chapter 4.

IV. Evaluation

The student may receive a final grade of S (Satisfactory) or U (Unsatisfactory). To earn an S and academic credit, __all__ course requirements must be fulfilled satisfactorily within the specified time. A grade of U earns no academic credit. Should the intern earn a grade of U, the intern's academic advisor, university supervisor, and intern will develop a remediation plan. The grades of S and U are not included in the computation of the grade point average.

V. Intern Performance Guidelines

- Avoid becoming involved in ideological disputes. The intern's role is participant-observer - - be objective.

- Confidentiality of records and of internal matters **must** be maintained at all times. Any violation of confidentiality will result in the termination of the internship with a grade of U.

- At the end of the second week of the internship, the intern will submit a school improvement project plan (see Appendix C) to the university supervisor. The field supervisor should assist the intern in selecting the problem to be addressed.

- Any behavior deemed improper (detrimental to the school or university) will result in termination of the internship with a grade of U.
- All materials submitted, except the daily log, must be typed.

- All materials submitted become the property of the Department of Educational Leadership.

- Professional dress is expected during the internship.

VI. Responsibilities of the Department of Educational Leadership

It shall be the responsibility of the Department to:

- Fully cooperate with school systems and agencies participating in the internship.

- Provide an university supervisor to coordinate activities.

- Provide information and mentor preparation session for field supervisors at beginning of each quarter/semester.

- Maintain regular contact with the intern's field supervisor on a monthly basis during the course of the internship to discuss the intern's progress. A contact report (see Appendix D) will be completed by the faculty supervisor and made part of the student's permanent internship file.

- Maintain regular contact with the intern on a monthly basis through site visitations. During these visits, the university supervisor will discuss progress on the mini-project, portfolio development, and other matters pertaining to the intern's professional development.

- Assist in the development of the intern's leadership portfolio.

- Develop appropriate and timely Saturday Seminars.

- Determine the intern's final grade.

- Notify the student if it becomes necessary to terminate the placement, and to explain why termination was necessary.

- Discuss termination with the field supervisor.

VII. Responsibilities of School Districts Accepting Interns

It shall be the responsibility of school districts to:

- Provide the intern with meaningful tasks and to insure exposure to as many operational and instructional leadership aspects as possible.

- Provide a supervisor to direct and coordinate the student's internship and to prepare a written evaluation of the intern's performance (see Appendix E).

- Offer intern constructive criticism when needed.

- Provide facilities, supplies, space, etc., which are necessary for the intern to adequately perform his or her assigned duties.

- Assist the intern in selection of a school improvement project.

- Alert the faculty supervisor of any problems relating to the intern's job performance.

- Request university supervisor to withdraw the intern when personal conduct or educational progress is such that additional time and effort on the part of the school district would not be worthwhile.

- Make suggestions to the university supervisor about how the internship program might be improved.

VIII. Techniques for Increasing Involvement between the University and School Systems

Techniques for increasing the involvement of all who participate in the internship are varied. The following are not suggested as a complete listing, however, they can be modified and added to based upon the situation.

At the close of the quarter/semester prior to the start of the internship, those who will be participating in the internship are required to submit their application for the internship. Upon receipt and approval of the application (see Appendix A), student is sent notice of the required introductory seminar (see Chapter 4). Included in this notification packet is a letter inviting their immediate supervisor and/or designee to attend this session. Through their attendance at the seminar, the various schools/systems contribute to the continuing evolution of the internship program.

Site visitations by the university field supervisor provide the university and school with a continuing dialog pertinent to internship development. These visits, as outlined above, occur on a monthly basis. The EDL Advisory Council provides for another school/university forum. This Council, comprised of practicing school and system-wide administrators, meets twice yearly to discuss current practices, recent trends, and future direction for the Department of Educational Leadership and the impact its programs and services have on local schools.

Another method of EDL/school involvement occurs in the operation of State Educational Service Agency/Consortium. In this forum, superintendents from local schools gather on a monthly basis to discuss common concerns and to hear presentations on a variety of education-related topics. One of these sessions is devoted to a dialog with several of the EDL faculty about ongoing practices in the Department of Educational Leadership as well as for the solicitation of system-wide needs. An outcome from this dialog may be the development of a principal's/superintendent's assessment center. These centers are designed to examine potential and current administrators on various aspects related to administrative leadership skills. A final outcome of these discussions may be the increased awareness on the parts of all participants for field-based action research.

IX. Benefits for the Intern, School Systems, and University

Benefits the intern accrues from his/her participation in the program include an opportunity to place theory into practice.   Through the internship, the individual gains insight into the everyday functioning of a school. Educational, social, and political influences of all of the school's publics are compared and contrasted from the perspective of administration. In addition, through the development of the portfolio and participation in the Saturday Seminars, the intern hones his/her skills in application and interviewing techniques. Finally, the internship provides the student with last opportunity to refine his/her leadership philosophy prior to accepting an entry level administrative position.

School system benefits from having personnel involved in the internship include the opportunity to assess the leadership potential of aspiring administrators. With the inclusion of the mini-project as a requirement for the internship, school administrators have the opportunity to assign a needed school improvement project to a competent individual. In addition the intern brings current theory/techniques to his/her school. Finally, in some cases, the university supervisor serves as an outside consultant to various programs and/or changes being considered by the school administrator.

The university and its personnel stay current with real-world school problems, concerns, and exemplary practices.   Through its involvement with participating schools, the university is able to make programmatic changes based on needs observed through the process. Lastly, the collaborative efforts of the university and schools can lead to continuing action-based research for the improvement of education at both levels.

CHAPTER 4

THE SATURDAY SEMINARS

When students are involved in an internship program, it is important that they not feel as though they are alone in the field; that they have an opportunity to converse with other interns who are experiencing some of the same challenges that they themselves encounter. In addition, it is important for the university's internship supervisors to present information to the interns in an atmosphere that resembles a classroom so that the interns can discuss the presented material with each other and their supervisors. Perhaps the most efficient method to achieve these goals is the Saturday Seminar.

A series of four seminars are slated for Saturday mornings, however, this number may be increased and topics added depending on the nature and length of the internship. The seminars are held on Saturdays so interns will not have to leave their schools prior to the end of the day to get to them and thus not be available to assist in some function at their school. Furthermore, the seminars are scheduled in advance so the interns can plan for substitute coverages if needed for any athletic events, music activities, or other school-based functions to which they have been assigned. At the beginning of the internship, the students are provided with the topics to be discussed in advance so they may arrive prepared to participate in a discussion format.

Suggested topics for the seminars include, but are not limited to: An Introduction to the Administrative Internship; Professionalism and Ethics; So You Want to be an Educational Leader; and a Saturday of Sharing (when the interns report to their peers on their internship projects and peer review portfolios--see Chapter 5). In addition to these topics, various case studies and simulations are introduced through an In-Basket format. These In-Baskets are presented during the second seminar (opening of school problems) and third Saturday seminar (closing of school problems). The interns are provided feedback to their responses to the various situations during the university supervisor's visit to the field (for In-Basket simulations see Section III, Chapter 5).

I. The First Seminar: An Introduction to the Administrative Internship

This first session is generally conducted prior to the start of the regular class schedule for the college or university. By doing this the intern can gain one or more weeks on needed administrative responsibility time for the internship (15 hours per week average). The field-based supervisor for the intern is encouraged to attend this session so he/she can develop a fuller understanding of the program. In addition, when the field-based supervisors attend this initial session with their intern, they have the opportunity to resolve any conflicts that may be apparent with the intern and his/her duties or responsibilities at the school.

The seminar begins with an introduction of the interns and their supervisors. This is followed by the university faculty presenting the various components of the program complete with the hourly requirements, acceptable and unacceptable internship projects, and the signing of various participation forms by the student and the field-based supervisor (see Appendix A). The area which tends to receive the most concern from everyone involved is the attainment of the 15 hours per week of administrative assignment, especially for those interns who are in the classroom and not already serving in an administrative capacity. All too often, this requirement has been relegated to three basic duties, i.e. before school bus duty, cafeteria duty, and after school bus duty. During the course of this opening seminar, the university supervisors need to stress that, as future administrators, the interns must become involved in the many facets of school management. Suggestions are made that include budget development/expenditure, curriculum revision, and discipline referrals to name three, any one of which could be expanded into the intern's school-based project for the course.

Following the discussion on the hourly expectations of the internship, the students are presented with their first examination of the internship portfolio and weekly log. The notion of developing a living document that will highlight an individual's career path toward and in administration is novel for many of the students and their field-based supervisors. However, at the university-level portfolios are becoming a method of faculty evaluation with designs toward promotion and tenure while in the public schools, portfolio evaluation is taking on more importance as various elementary and middle level schools look to the development of portfolios as a means of developing a qualitative approach to student assessment.

Time is allotted at the conclusion of the session for the university-based supervisor, the school-based supervisor, and the intern to meet and become acquainted. In addition, the university-based supervisor uses this time to schedule visits to the intern at his/her school. Finally, the meeting is used to lay the foundation for a successful internship experience. These activities comprise the first of the series of Saturday seminars.

II. Seminar Two: Professionalism and Ethics

The second of the Saturday seminars is divided into two distinct areas--professional dress and ethics, and the completion of the first of two in-basket activities. In the first of these--professional dress and ethics--much of the students coursework throughout the certification process has focused on the content and process of administration. Very little time has been devoted to either or both of these areas. The first of area--professional dress--however, is what makes that first impression at the interview and is the image seen by the public while the second area--ethics--is what may, at times, make the difference between a successful career and one that is marred by controversy--student, faculty, and support staff.

Professional Dress

Interns are often times oblivious to their dress and the dress of their colleagues. All one has to do is walk into any public school and try to determine who is on the professional staff and who are the students. When a person is the administrator of a school, he/she is the individual who establishes the atmosphere of the learning environment. If the administrator is carefree and unkempt, the school will reflect that attitude. However, if the administrator is meticulous to detail and sharp in his/her appearance, the likelihood of the school reflecting those values is great.

Included in the discussion of professional dress is the entire picture the public sees. It is interesting to observe the manner in which school administrators who dress as professionals are received by the business community as compared to those administrators who are seen in public attired in blue jeans and collarless shirts. As our schools are constantly compared to business models and as school/business partnerships are continuously stressed, school leaders must begin to take on the appearance of a properly attired manager. There are, however, times when spirit days or pep rallies beckon administrators to shed their dress clothes for apparel more becoming of the events. At these times a second set of clothes should be carefully placed in the office closet so that following the event, the administrator can return to his/her professional appearance.

Interns are informed that they are professionals and should dress accordingly. Many times this comes as a surprise, especially to the athletic coach or industrial arts teacher who is accustomed to much more casual attire. In these instances, the interns are requested to dress for their teaching position (safety requirements are especially important for industrial arts teachers) but should be prepared to don professional dress when involved in performing any of their administrative duties. This is when area which is noted by the university supervisors when they visit interns in the field. Since information about professional image, dress, and interviewing is not readily available, a rather detailed description of this part of the seminar is included.

Developing the Professional Image. How often we all hear the expression clothes make the man yet in our profession we tend to ignore the importance of dress for professional success. To succeed in any field one must establish credibility quickly. This is especially true of education.

Importance of Professional Image. For some unknown reasons educators often believe that professional dress applies to only doctors, nurses, attorneys, bank tellers and flight attendants. We fail to let professional dress help us every day in the classroom or school office. Every time we walk into a class room or school building we make a visual impression on our students, parents, administrators, and other staff members.

Consider the following scenarios: the first scene is a middle school classroom with the teacher dressed in jeans, tennis shoes, and open collared shirt who is working at his desk during his planning period. The office secretary informs him via the intercom that Mrs. Jones is on her way down to his room to discuss her son's grades. In the second scene the only difference is that the teacher is wearing a fresh pressed pair of khaki pants, a long sleeved light blue shirt with a conservative dark blue tie with perhaps a pair of well-polished loafers. Who do you think will immediately establish credibility in the first few seconds of the meeting? You can, of course, see the difference. The professionally dressed teacher immediately makes a statement of professional presence. Because of his dress, he appears believable.

In the first scene the teacher must first work to establish the parent's confidence through his speaking because the impression of his dress will tend not to make his position creditable to the parent. Professional educators, teachers and administrators, are role models to our students as well as their parents. Much of what is included in this image is in our professional appearance. In our own work settings, educators need to be able to convey an "I am the educator," the person in charge of this classroom/school and I am a positive role model for your child.

How to Begin. Those who aspire to educational leadership often ask the question, "Where and how do I begin?" Naturally, one must attend graduate school and earn the degree and/or state certificate. But prior to that, aspiring administrators can begin by dressing the part. Wear the uniform of a school leader even while in the classroom. When this is done people will begin to see you as an administrator if you take on the garb of the title. School leaders should dress their part as they meet countless individuals from all walks of life. Through appropriate dress these school leaders can immediately establish a creditable base. It is important to let your appearance work **for** you rather than against you. It is the first step in letting others know you are an aspiring administrator.

The Administrator Uniform. A few of the essentials included in the administrative uniform include the following:
Males:
Well pressed slacks in navy, gray, black or khaki become the foundation of the male administrative uniform. The belt and shoes should be brown, black, or cordovan and should match. In particular, a brown or plain leather belt is preferable. Current style also has braces as acceptable; however, when wearing braces, stay with solid colors that are coordinated to the rest of the attire. Shoes should either be well cared for, solid colored, dress loafers or wing tips. Although other varieties of shoes may be a bit more comfortable, the overall appearance dictates these two styles. The shirt should be long sleeved, regardless of the outdoor temperature, and in either a solid white or blue. Emphasis is placed on the sleeve length because as a leader, you will be required to have a suit/sport coat on at various times during the day and at those times, the sleeve should extend approximately one-half inch past the end of the coat sleeve. The tie should be a coordinated tie with a small detail print. It is important that you have with you a coordinated sport coat or matching suit coat to be worn as the situation dictates.

Depending on the particular day at your school, you may find it necessary to have a pair of blue jeans, t-shirt and/or sweat shirt, and a pair of sneakers available. However, it must be noted that this attire is unacceptable when presenting yourself as the "Leader" of the school.

Females:

Two choices present themselves for females. These are two piece suits in solid colors such as navy or gray (a first choice) or a dark solid skirt, white or light colored shirt or dress blouse, and a blazer in navy, black, or charcoal. When the weather becomes warmer a wheat colored suit or blazer will work well. A plain low-heeled polished pump is non-trendy and helps one navigate the halls. It is also recommended that a very low heel be worn because administrators must be able to get to places quickly should an emergency arise. Hosiery can be natural or light tan depending on the season.

The best method to increase your image is to wear the conservative colors of navy, charcoal, or black. These are considered the power colors. Forest green, dark brown or taupe are also acceptable in skirts, blouses and blazers. Women can also wear coat dresses or other executive type dresses usually in solid colors.

Females need to avoid pinks unless it is under a black suit. Many schools have uneven heating, however, the wearing of sweaters portray the image of a secretary. When flowers are worn, the send the message that you are not in charge. The practice of wearing heavy jewelry should be avoided since this tends to indicate a glitzy a individual.

Many times, elementary administrators occasionally wear jumpers or blouses decorated with school prints, apples, or other school decorations on them. Limit this type of clothing to special occasions. It can be difficult to establish a leadership sense of presence with parents or other system administrators with this type clothing. However, if you plan to visit an elementary class for a special occasion, this type of clothing is acceptable.

The Job Interview. You have just received the most anticipated call concerning your career. The personnel director has contacted you about your application for an administrative position in a quality school system. An interview has been scheduled for the following week. The way in which you present yourself during this interview will determine if you have cleared the first hurdle in securing an administrative position or the last opportunity you will have for such a position in that school system.

Plan to wear a conservative solid navy, gray, or black suit with conservative shoes in a coordinated color. Do not mix blue clothing with black shoes. Good grooming is a must. Plan a hair appointment immediately. This is important for men and women if adjustments in style are necessary after the first visit or to avoid that noticeable fresh hair cut look. You should not only be well groomed, but carry a natural appearance.

Nails are an important item for men and women and a neatly manicured appearance is important. A light color polish that is coordinated with the apparel is the best bet for women. Jewelry for both men and women should be kept to a minimum. For men, a watch (preferably not a plastic athletic watch) and a wedding ring are sufficient. A woman can wear a watch, ring, small earrings, and one necklace, perhaps pearls, or thin gold chain. Above all, you do not want to be remembered for your jewelry.

Both men and women need to keep fragrances to a bare minimum, preferably in a clean scent. Florals tend to become sweet, thereby taking away from your presentation. You do not want your fragrance to arrive before you or overshadow your responses during the interview.

Practice in your mind how you will walk into the interviewer's office keeping in mind the need to make a smooth entrance with an even stride. Walk into the interview in a confident fashion and stand tall. Good posture exhibits a businesslike character, and the "I'm in control" attitude.

Upon entering, shake hands and establish eye contact. Introduce yourself by using your name, and using the name(s) of the person(s) interviewing you by thanking them for the opportunity to discuss this potential position. Following the introductions, it is advisable to be seated and wait for the interviewer to initiate the interview process. During the interview it is a must to sit tall and maintain an air of confidence. Remember, **you** are administrative material, your dress, posture, and behavior will say this.

Role play ahead of time possible questions and answers. This is not the time to try and be totally spontaneous. To assist you in this preparation, investigate ahead of time the school system, the community, and the school. In addition, develop an internalized knowledge and belief system based on the following questions which will most likely be asked during your interview:

1. What is your philosophy of education?
2. What are the 3 most important issues presently facing education?
3. What strengths do you have that will benefit this school/system?
4. Discuss your weaknesses and what you are doing or plan to do to compensate for these?
5. Why should we choose you over the other candidates?
6. Where will you be and what will you be doing years from now.

It is imperative to look at the person who asked the question when you begin giving your answers. During the answer, look at the other interviewers while occasionally smiling. Your answers should always be up-beat and positive. If you do not understand the question, ask the interviewer to repeat or rephrase the question. Do not attempt to bluff your way through a question for which you do not know the answer.

If the interviewer asks if you can take on a project or develop an idea that you have not yet tried, be positive and suggest in a reassuring manner that you are capable and willing to work for the betterment of the school, system, and community. Remember...there has not been a major project that you have undertaken that you failed to accomplish.

The most effective method of demonstrating competence on the job aside from your curriculum vita is through the development of a portfolio. If you have not developed a portfolio, now is the time to begin. The portfolio focuses the interview and ensuing discussion from you the person to your demonstrated work and activities. It is important to keep your portfolio sharing short and pointed to one or two particular items unless the interviewer shows interest in other components. This is done to highlight rather than take over the interview.

Make a conscious effort to be aware of your gestures before the interview. Concentrate on keeping small, close to the body gestures. Large, exaggerated moves speak of unpolished, manual type laborers. Small, controlled gestures suggest, refinement and culture.

Keep your voice low at all times. Practice ahead of time voice control by humming "mumm," "mumm," and "mumm." A conscious effort to take a full breath of air and lower the voice prior to speaking will result in a voice that is resonant and pleasant.

Standard American English is an absolute **must** during the interview. Tape record various discussions in which you are involved and analyze what you hear or have someone else listen and provide you with honest feedback. Unless you do this, no one else will be willing to critique your speech habits. Since speaking is a part of the personal self it is rare when polite people correct colleagues or friends when they make a spoken error in grammar. Borrow a basic grammar book and practice the use of the correct English. One grammatical error during the interview can be deadly to an aspiring administrator. School personnel must know that you can communicate correctly and effectively with parents and the various publics. You will also be part of the administrative staff, the leadership of the school system--one speaks for many.

Summary

The aspiring educational leader must realize that skills, abilities, and academic preparation alone will not guarantee a leadership position. Superintendents and boards of education look for these skills as well as for the public image a person presents. School leadership requires role models who are a cut above the rest and are willing to bring out the best in everyone.

ETHICS

"PARENTS ENTRUST THE CARE OF THEIR CHILDREN TO EDUCATORS."
These are very powerful words that imply a contract with an enormous responsibility for educational leaders. There is a professional obligation and a duty implied to uphold this unwritten contract with school clients. Parents have the right to expect that their children are in the care of a professional who practice and maintain a standard of exemplary conduct. To this end, it is the responsibility of graduate schools of preparation and the leadership student to internalize a code of ethical behavior. Therefore, the purpose of this section is set into motion an understanding of ethics and to ensure student exposure to examples of codes of ethical conduct.

Some Assumptions. Students who are accepted into graduate programs for leadership certification, generally have undergraduate degrees or certification in an area of education and have classroom or student services-related experiences. These individuals are making a commitment to be a role model in the school and community. It should be assumed that these future leaders have internalized a code of ethics that will distinguish them from others in the teaching or service-related ranks. However, too often this is not the case. Many individuals aspiring to be educational leaders are unaware of ethical codes of behavior and demonstrate few professional behaviors.

Educators and Professionalism. Educators have consistently viewed themselves as professionals. They expect to be treated as professionals and ask for salaries commensurate with other professionals. Educators have professional organizations, professional journals, professional codes of ethics (see Appendix F), and licensing requirements by the various states. The question can then be asked: Why is it that educators continue to have difficulty being recognized as professionals within the community and by other professionals? Three reasons are suggested for this lack of acceptance.

First, educators do not have a standard code of ethics they recognize and to which they take an oath to uphold. This is a common practice of the other professions with which educators equate status. There are codes of ethics for educators, but for whatever reason, there has been a reluctance on the part of educational organizations to embrace these codes either individually or collectively.

Secondly, if an educator is accused of violating an ethical behavior, the professional organization does not bring the individual before his/her peers for a review and for the administration of sanctions if found guilty of having committed a violation. Rather, the professional education organizations for both teachers and administrators often provides a defense for the educator against the charges.

Thirdly, certifying agencies are not consistent in the practice of requiring the successful completion of a state examination before receiving a license to practice. Each state determines what school and/or system levels require certification and what requirements are necessary. There is at least one state which requires no certificate for being an educational leader.

In the absence of these requirements and the lack of consistency between governing bodies, it is the responsibility of the individual student, the student's school system, and the his/her graduate school of education to assist in the internalizing of a code of ethics that is reflected in both personal and professional behaviors.

Codes of Ethics. Internship seminars provide the opportunity for future leaders to examine and discuss a variety of codes of ethics. The interns should have the opportunity to discuss teacher specific, leadership specific, and comprehensive codes of ethics. Following the examination of the codes of ethics, interns should be given the opportunity through case studies and in-basket activities to make informed ethical decisions concerning their leadership roles (see Chapter 5 for case studies and in-basket activities).

III. Seminar Three: So You Want to be an Educational Leader

Within the field of public school education, there are little means for an individual to gain advancement without entering the ranks of leadership. Higher education has various entry levels for its faculties, and businesses have various entry levels for their employees. However, in public education individuals gain advancement through only three means. The first of these is by acquiring additional degrees or credits towards degrees. Through negotiated contracts or system pay schedules, teachers advance on a salary schedule as they accrue advanced work in their chosen field. A second way public school teachers can gain advancement is through the length of their tenure within a particular school or system. This comes about through either a negotiated year-by-year salary increase or a salary schedule within the system or state. If one can envision a graph with credits/degrees along the horizontal and years experience along the vertical, all one has to do is determine the years experience on the vertical and move across the horizontal to the appropriate level of credits/degree to determine a salary. There is virtually no way to financially reward meritorious work, the development of new curricula, innovative teaching methods, or extra time given to assist students. Additional monies may be obtained for items such as athletic coaching, musical direction, team leadership, or club sponsors, however, these additional funds, in the form of salary stipends, are seldom calculated into the base salary of the individual. Therefore, when the teacher ceases to sponsor a stipend-producing activity, their salary reverts to their base of years of service and credit/degree earned.

The final method available to teachers to advance in the education is to move from the classroom to the administrative office. However, when interviewing beginning graduate students about the motivation for them to enter an Educational Leadership Program, many of them indicate that their primary reason for making the change from teacher to leader is based on finances. Although the increase in salary is definitely a plus for the move from teacher to leader, it should not be the driving force. The purpose of this seminar is to bring to the intern the realities of school leadership; insight from those who are or who have been school leaders.

Throughout their internship, these individuals will be involved in their teaching assignments and will not have an adequate opportunity to see the inner workings of educational leadership. As the seminar is designed, former and current leaders from elementary, middle, and high school are brought together to give the interns a view from the inside of the day-to-day operations in a school. This provides a supplement to the Shadow Experience which is required of every intern during their internship (see Chapter 3).

In discussing the role of the educational leader, it is important to stress the hours that are demanded by the job. Although leaders are not held accountable for the hours they are at school, they are expected to be the first one there in the morning and the last one to leave in the afternoon. This, of course, does not include days when there are school board meetings, parent meetings, or other school-related functions the school leader is expected to attend.

Another area that needs to be examined carefully is the misconception that when school is out for the summer (or on vacation) nothing is taking place. It is during these periods of school closing that much of the work takes place that permits the school to run smoothly. Included in this is the development of the master schedule, the ordering of supplies and textbooks, and interviewing substitute and replacement teachers to name only a few.

Perhaps the most difficult task the leader will have to handle involves evaluation of faculty and staff. Many interns profess a desire to move into a leadership role within the school or system in which they are currently teaching. Although this is a noble thought, it may be one of the most stressful assignments an administrator could ever attempt. As a teacher, the intern is one of a group of professionals working together to instruct students in various content areas, however, once that individual crosses into a leadership role, he/she is now in a position to evaluate, reprimand, and in some instances terminate an individual with whom they had taught. Friendships that had seemed inseparable now are viewed in a different light. The new school leader will become privy to information that is not available to his/her former colleagues and may become involved in matters relating to the effectiveness of faculty members or the personal lives of students. These items should not be shared with even the closet of friends for in the event that the information is leaked, lives and careers may be permanently damaged.

The culminating activity to this seminar is done by grouping the students according to their areas of expertise, i.e. elementary, middle, or high school. In light of their experiences and the information they have gained thus far during their internship, they are asked to list three concerns for their division and to develop goals and objectives to confront and resolve these concerns. They are given seminar time to arrive at these solutions and then are required to select one individual to present the division's report to the class as a whole. Time is provided for feedback from both the professors and members from other divisions.

As the students prepare to leave this third seminar, they are handed a packet containing their second and final in-basket. This in-basket contains situations that arise toward the end of an academic year. The students are informed that their in-basket responses will be discussed during the final visit from their university supervisor.

IV. Seminar Four: Project Presentation, Peer Portfolio Review, and Internship
      Evaluation

The fourth and final seminar is based around the interns and their work during the quarter/semester. This session is designed for the presentation and sharing of the interns' mini project, an overview of their internship experience, and a peer review of their portfolios. Each intern is required to make a 10-15 minute presentation of his/her experiences, complete with keyed handouts. Within this presentation, the intern must discuss the various functions and duties performed, an analysis of the mini-project conducted, a reflection on the school board meetings attended, and a comparison of the leadership styles observed--from the field-based supervisor and the person shadowed. After each presentation, fellow interns and university professors are encouraged to interact with the intern about material presented.

Following the conclusion of the presentations, the students are presented with a peer evaluation form (see Appendix I) to be used as they review each other's portfolios. Each intern is required to review two portfolios and submit their completed evaluation forms to the instructors. This process is used let the interns see another individual's portfolio. Since the portfolio which is developed during the internship is a living document, upon seeing something unique in a peer's work can look for ways to include such information in their ongoing portfolio development.

At the conclusion of this seminar, the students are provided an opportunity to evaluate their internship experience through a university-designed instrument. The instrument (see Appendix J) contains a Likert scale assessment followed by several areas for student qualitative responses. It is through these assessment procedures that the internship program continually evolves.

V. Other Possible Seminar Topics

It is advisable to have several other topics for seminars. Since the seminars are examined by administrative assignment i.e. elementary, middle, or high school, it is important to bring topics to this seminar that cross division lines. Examples of possible topics include:
   The Impact of Special Education Law
   State Curriculum Guidelines
   Targeted Selection
   Conflict Resolution
   Stress Management
   Parent and Community Relations
   Multicultural Considerations
   Technology for the Administrator
   School-to-Work Initiatives
   School Improvement Plans
   Teacher Empowerment

These topics are rather precise and the use of an outside resource people may prove helpful.

SECTION III:

PERFORMANCE ASSESSMENT

The purpose of this section is to provide information on techniques for evaluating the leadership skills of the intern. A brief discussion of the purposes of in-baskets and case studies is presented. A current trend in education is portfolio development. Provided in this section is information on how to develop the portfolio narrative and the types of support evidence that should be considered for inclusion.

Chapter 5
Skills Assessment

I. In-Baskets

The use of in-basket simulations (see Appendix G) within the Saturday Seminar format is used to assist the perspective leader develop an insight into the thought process associated with educational leadership. This process is used to assist the intern in developing a sense of connectedness between his/her classroom work and actual practice. In addition, the constraint of time has been added to the in-basket simulation to give the intern an example of the limited time associated with many educational decisions. Although there are no right or wrong answers to the simulations, each has been derived from actual events.

II. Case Studies

The view an individual takes on an issue is influenced by that person's position relative to the issue. Teachers are likely to view educational concerns from a different perspective than leadership. The internship places the intern in close proximity to leaders and their decisions. This provides the intern with an opportunity to reflect upon what action was taken and what he/she may have done differently. Often times, the internship does not provide ample opportunities for first hand critical decision making, therefore, it is necessary to provide additional opportunities.

The case study approach is an effective tool in practicing decision making skills. Case studies in leadership provide the intern with real and potential situations he/she may encounter as a school leader. This is an opportunity for reflective practice where theory and knowledge can be enacted without the consequences.

The case studies in Appendix H were taken from actual school events. Questions are provided to give a variety of perspectives on the issue. A response should be developed for each question that can be defended by the intern. Additional questions may be developed for each case.

III. The Leadership Portfolio

The recent movement toward portfolio assessment has been felt by both students and teachers. Now, in this time of accountability, the movement is extending to include educational leaders. According to Edgerton, Hutching, and Quinlan (1991), portfolios are a step toward a public, professional view of education.

This section guides both the intern and the university supervisor through the steps of portfolio preparation. Field supervisors interested in preparing a portfolio, for self-evaluation or as part of a district evaluation plan, should also find the information beneficial. The information presented should also prove valuable to school districts moving toward portfolio assessment for their administrators.

What is the leadership portfolio?

The leadership portfolio is a portrait, depicting the strengths and weaknesses of the individual preparing it. Included are documents and materials that collectively suggest the scope and quality of the educational leader's administrative style. It enables administrators to display their leadership accomplishments for others to examine.

Portfolios take the assessment process past a hierarchical, often standardized evaluation system because evidence is provided from a variety of sources. It is important to remember that the portfolio is not an exhaustive compilation of all of the documents related to administration. Rather, it includes selected information from course work, leadership activities, and internship experiences. The intended outcome is solid evidence of effectiveness (Seldin, 1993).

Why prepare an leadership portfolio?

There are five basic reasons for the preparation of the leadership portfolio. First, it is a mechanism for providing hard evidence of completion of the 12 guidelines outlined in Chapter 2. It enables the university supervisor to assess an intern's strengths, weaknesses, and progress toward professional knowledge. Second, it is a useful tool for presenting evidence of leadership experiences in a practical and efficient manner during an interview. The ability to provide hard evidence to a perspective employer is indispensable. Third, interns have reported that it contributes to their professional self-confidence. The portfolio serves as a set of "tools" that the administrative intern can carry with them as they progress in their career. Fourth, it enables the Educational Leadership Department to analyze the effects of the leadership program on the development of interns related to the goals and objectives of the educational leadership program. The faculty gains a deeper understanding of strengths and weaknesses of the program. Identified program weakness can be targeted for improvement. Fifth, and perhaps most important, the portfolio allows the individual to reflect on their beliefs, convictions, and accomplishments for the purposes of self improvement. The process of portfolio development should cause the intern to deeply consider their leadership philosophy and their beliefs about teaching and learning. These reflections should lead to improvement in performance.

What goes in an leadership portfolio?

There are two parts to an leadership portfolio. First is the narrative, which is a reflective document detailing such areas as the leadership and teaching/learning philosophy, leadership responsibilities, accomplishments, and improvement activities. Usually the narrative is eight to ten pages in length. Described within the narrative is what and why the intern leads others as he or she does. The leadership narrative must reflect consistency between beliefs about leadership and the intern's actions in school. Sample narratives are provided in Appendix I.

The second part of the leadership portfolio is the appendix. All claims made in the narrative must be supported by evidence in the appendices. Major attention must focus on evidence supporting effective leadership.

Is collaboration important in developing the portfolio?

The portfolio process requires individual guidance by a person familiar with the process. Credibility of the portfolio is increased through the supervisory support system. The university supervisor should guide the writing process and selection of supportive evidence. Together the intern and the professor critically analyze the leadership philosophy and career objectives of the intern. They decide what types of information remain to be collected and how best to present the information developed and obtained. The university supervisor must help the intern understand that portfolio development is not the collection of a "bunch of stuff" from their desk and filing cabinet but a way to analyze leadership performance for self improvement in an effort to obtain career objectives. Portfolio development should be seen as a learning experience for both the intern and the university supervisor.

How does one begin the portfolio narrative?

It is recommended that the intern begin the process of developing the narrative by answering the reflective questions listed in Appendix I. These questions provide the ground work for deciding what to include in the actual narrative. Once the questions are completed, the university supervisor reviews each response for content and to provide the intern with direction on how to proceed with writing the narrative. The university supervisor gains a deeper understanding of what the intern believes and why they lead as they do. Often students want to skip laying the ground work as they find some questions difficult to answer; however, without answers to these questions it is extremely difficult to write the narrative.

What headings might be used in the narrative?

It is important to recognize that each portfolio yields a unique portrait of the individual compiling it. The list below provides suggested narrative headings. Each intern should feel free to use or combine any of these or none of these. Other headings, which are developed by the intern and their university supervisor, may better suit the intern's purposes.

Possible narrative headings:

Leadership Philosophy	Improvement Activities
Teaching and Learning Philosophy	Future Leadership Goals/Directions
Administrative Responsibilities	Awards and Recognition
Description of Leadership Practices	Assessment of Effectiveness
Analysis of Leadership Techniques, Strategies	

<u>Which items should be selected for inclusion in the portfolio appendices?</u>

First, it is extremely important to select items which provide evidence for the portfolio narrative. The items chosen should be applicable to both the leadership and teaching responsibilities of the intern. Items which may be selected include outstanding lessons developed, student work, grants written, agendas prepared, memos written, revised policies, forms created, conference presentations, etc.. These items must be direct products of the intern.

Next, the intern should include course work from their leadership preparation program. Prior to portfolio implementation, the Leadership Department should meet to determine which assignments are to be included in the portfolio. It is preferable to select key assignments that reflect broad areas of student knowledge which are included in the leadership areas discussed in Chapter 2. Students should be informed prior to completion of the assignment, that it is to be included in their leadership portfolio. Also, to be included here would be activities completed during the internship.

Finally, information obtained from others should be included. This would include evaluation information which reflects areas of strength and/or suggestions for improvement. Supportive statements from colleagues who are knowledgeable of educational contributions made by the intern should also be included. Additional information which should be included consist of notes from students and honors or awards received by the intern.

<u>What sections should be included in the appendices?</u>

Much like the narrative headings, appendix sections vary from portfolio to portfolio; however, there are a few sections that should be considered standard. Course work selected to be included in the portfolio should appear in the Guideline which it best represents. Recommended sections include:

Professional and Ethical Leadership
Information Management and Evaluation
Instructional Leadership
Professional Development and Human Resources
Student Personnel Services
Organizational Management
Interpersonal Relationships
Financial Management and Resource Allocation
Technology and Information Systems
Community and Media Relations
Educational Law, Public Policy and Political Systems
Examples of Exemplary Teaching
Workshop/Conference Information
Scholarly Products (if applicable)
Funded Grants
Information from Others (leadership/teaching)
Resume

How might the leadership portfolio be evaluated?

It is recommended that each portfolio be review by a panel consisting of the supervising professor and one or two other department members. This will allow for the analysis to be based on inter-rater reliability. An interesting concept, is to have each intern evaluate the portfolios of two other interns, during the last seminar. This not only gives the intern experience at portfolio evaluation, but also allows them to gain ideas on other types of information that they may wish to include in their own portfolio. Within Appendix I is a form which provides possible criteria to use in the overall evaluation of the leadership portfolio.

How often should the portfolio be updated?

The portfolio should be consider a living document; therefore, it should be updated at least annually. Updating is based on individual preference and necessity. It is recommended that the intern keep an evidence folder in their desk. Each time they complete a task that is representative of their narrative or have something come across their desk that is worthy of inclusion in their portfolio, it should be placed in the folder. Time should be set aside on the educational leader's personal calendar to update their portfolio.

Should the entire portfolio be taken on a job interview?

The portfolio compiled for the internship should be considered a "master" from which to pull. Information to take on a job interview should be selected with care, after a thorough examination of the job description for which the individual has applied. The information selected, along with the leader narrative and resume, should be placed in a leather portfolio. This will enhance the professional image.

IV. Summary

It is important for the intern, field supervisor, and university supervisor to evaluate the total internship experience both individually and collaboratively. This includes reviewing field experiences, seminar participation, and assessment materials. The intended end result is an educational leader who possess both the knowledge base and skills to be an effective leader.

Appendix A

Internship Admission and Acceptance Forms

(NAME OF UNIVERSITY)
DEPARTMENT OF EDUCATIONAL LEADERSHIP
INTERNSHIP IN EDUCATIONAL LEADERSHIP

Application for Internship

Date: _____

Name: _____

Social Security Number: _____ Student ID Number: _____

Home Address: _____

City: _____ State: _____ Phone: _____

School Name: _____

School Address: _____

City: _____ State: _____ Phone: _____

Position: _____ Years in Current Position: _____

Total Years Teaching Experience: _____

Available time for visitations: _____

Career Goal: _____

Quarter/Semester of Expected Graduation: Fall   Winter   Spring   Summer

List grade or indicate current enrollment in core courses.

_____   _____   _____   _____

List required leadership courses completed and those of current enrollment:

COURSE	GRADE	COURSE	GRADE

Master's GPA: _____
Advisor's Approval Signature (for enrollment in the Internship): _____

DRAW A MAP TO YOUR PLACE OF EMPLOYMENT ON THE BACK OF THIS FORM.
BE SPECIFIC!!!

(Name of University)
Department of Educational Leadership

Student Agreement

I understand that I am participating in an internship sponsored by the Department of Educational Leadership and a school district. I recognize that in the internship I am subject to the rules, regulations and policies of (Name of University), as well as those that the field supervisor deems appropriate for the school system.

I understand that I am not covered by (Name of University) fringe benefits and that it is my responsibility to make arrangements for my own insurance, including accident, health, and hospitalization coverage. I will not hold (Name of University) liable for injury or death as a result of this internship.

I understand that in the internship I will be representing both (Name of University) and the Department of Educational Leadership; I will do nothing that would adversely affect the image of either unit. I agree that if any of my behavior is deemed improper, detrimental to the school system or (Name of University), I will withdraw from the internship and accept a grade of Unsatisfactory (U).

I understand that failure to abide by the policies and procedures of the internship program will result in termination of the internship with a grade of U.

I further agree that I will:

a.   Avoid becoming involved in ideological disputes.
b.   Maintain the confidentiality of records and internal matters at all times.
c.   Not be in possession of or use any item which is considered a controlled substance (except under the direction of a physician), alcohol, or firearm, while on school or university property, during my internship.
d.   Always dress professionally for the internship.

I HAVE READ THIS AGREEMENT. THE NATURE, SCOPE AND POLICIES OF THE INTERNSHIP PROGRAM HAVE BEEN EXPLAINED TO ME, AND I AGREE TO ABIDE BY THEM.

_____

Student

_____

University Supervisor   Date

IMMEDIATE SUPERVISOR
STATEMENT OF ACCEPTANCE FOR
INTERNSHIP IN EDUCATIONAL LEADERSHIP

I hereby approve _____ for an internship during   Fall

Winter   Spring   Quarter/Semester 19___, and agree to assist with his/her field

experiences. I understand that the internship involves a variety of administrative and

supervisory experiences on-site in a school or central office setting.

I am willing to work with this intern and the (Name of University) supervising

professor from the Department of Educational Leadership in developing an appropriate

set of experiences and a school improvement project.

_____
Signature of Immediate Supervisor

FIELD SUPERVISOR INFORMATION

Name of Field Supervisor: _____

Name of School: _____ District: _____

Degree Held: _____ Certification: _____

Current Position: _____ Years Experience: _____

Type of Teacher and/or Leadership Evaluation Preparation: _____

Mentor Preparation: ____ Yes ____ No

Appendix B

Weekly Log of Internship Experiences

Educational Leadership
Internship Experiences Checklist

Student Name: _____

Week: _____

Day of Week	Time	Area I Strategic Leadership		Area II Instructional Leadership			Area III Organizational Leadership				Area IV Pol and Comm Leadership	
		1. Prof and Ethical	2. Info Mngmnt/ Evaluation	3. Curr, Instruction, Supervision	4. Prof Dev & Hum Res	5. Student Personnel Services	6. Organizational Management	7. Interpersonal Relationships	8. Financial Manage & Res Alloc	9. Technology & Information Systems	10. Comm & Media Relations	11. Ed Law, Policy, Political Sys
Monday												
Tuesday												
Wednesday												

Thursday

Friday

R=Responsible
P=Participated
O=Observed

Total Hours Completed _____

Guidelines-See Chapter 2 for additional information

AREA I: Strategic Leadership
1.   Professional and Ethical Leadership
2.   Information Management and Evaluation

AREA II: Instructional Leadership
3.   Curriculum, Instruction, Supervision, and the Learning Environment
4.   Professional Development
5.   Student Personnel Services

AREA III: Organizational Leadership
6.   Organizational Management
7.   Interpersonal Relationships
8.   Financial Management and Resource Allocation
9.   Technology and Information Systems

AREA IV: Political and Community Leadership
10. Public Relations
11. Educational Law, Public Policy and Political Systems

Appendix C

School Improvement Project Plan

School Improvement Project Plan

Name: _____   Quarter/Semester: _____

School or System: _____

Position: _____

Specific area of focus of project: _____

Objective(s):

Activities/Procedures to be used:

Evaluation System:

Appendix D

Contact Report

(Name of University)
Department of Educational Leadership
Internship in Educational Leadership

Contact Log

Intern: _____

Date of Contact: _____ Person(s) Contacted: _____

Location: _____

Comments: _____

_____

_____

_____

_____

_____

_____

_____

_____

_____

_____

_____

_____

University Supervisor: _____

Appendix E

Performance Evaluation

(Name of University)
Department of Educational Leadership
Internship
Evaluation of Student Intern

Student: _____ Quarter/Semester: _____

Field Supervisor: _____

School: _____

Please use the chart below in evaluating the performance of the student who has interned in your school. Upon completion of this evaluation form, it should be returned to the university supervisor, by the field supervisor.

	Superior	Above Average	Average	Below Average	Unsatis-factory	Unable to Observe
Punctuality						
Attendance						
Appropriate Attire						
Cooperation						
Community Involvement						
Ability to Organize and Perform Assignments						
Problem Analysis						
Decisiveness						
Ability to use Supervision (seek and use help, accept criticism)						
Personal Motivation						
Judgment						
Written Communication						
Oral Communication						
Sensitivity						
Ability to Relate to Certified Personnel						
Stress Tolerance						
Ability to Relate to Non-Certified Personnel						
Ability to Relate to Students						
Educational Values						
Range of Interests						
Overall Performance						

Please comment on any other aspects of the student's internship performance.

_____

_____

_____

_____

Brief description of intern assignments: _____

_____

_____

Note: This evaluation will be kept confidential. Please return this evaluation to:

_____

University Intern Supervisor

_____

Signature of Field Supervisor

_____

Date

Appendix F

The AASA Code of Ethics

THE AASA CODE OF ETHICS

Policy 1

The professional school administrator constantly upholds the honor and dignity of his profession in all his actions and relations with pupils, colleagues, school board members, and the public.

Policy 2

The professional school administrator obeys local, state, and national laws; Holds himself to high ethical and moral standards, and gives loyalty to his country and to the cause of democracy and liberty.

Policy 3

The professional school administrator accepts the responsibility throughout his career to master and to contribute to the growing body of specialized knowledge, concepts, and skills which characterize school administration as a profession.

Policy 4

The professional school administrator strives to provide the finest possible educational experiences and opportunities to all persons in the district.

Policy 5

The professional school administrator applying for a position or entering into contractual agreements seeks to preserve and enhance the prestige and status of his profession.

Policy 6

The professional school administrator carries out in good faith all policies duly adopted by the local board and the regulations of state authorities and renders professional service to the best of his ability.

Policy 7

The professional school administrator honors the public trust of his position above any economic or social rewards.

Policy 8

The professional school administrator does not permit considerations of private gain nor personal economic interest to affect the discharge of his professional responsibilities.

Policy 9

The professional school administrator recognizes that the public schools are the public's business and seeks to keep the public fully and honestly informed about their schools.

Overview

High standards of ethical behavior for the professional school administrator are essential and are compatible with his faith in the power of public education and his commitment to leadership in the preservation and strengthening of the public schools.

Reprinted from The AASA Code of Ethics with permission from AASA

APPENDIX G
In-Basket Assessments

Beginning of the Year

In-Basket I

Background

You are Dr. Smith, and you are beginning the first day of your first year as principal of Hill Top School. It is Monday morning, August 16th, less than one week before the students return. Your faculty, all of whom were hired by your predecessor, Mr. Wells, will be coming back over the next two days to ready their rooms for the start of school and in preparation for their three days of pre-planning meetings. You are about to check your mail and any telephone messages. You have been out of town since Wednesday evening as the result of a family emergency.

Instructions

1. You will be given 75 minutes to read and take action on all of the in-basket items presented following the instructions. You are not expected merely to describe what you would do, but to do it. For example, if you decide to write a letter, then compose the letter. If you decide to telephone an individual or have a conference with someone, then outline your objectives, as well as the main points or questions that you would present.

2. Each of the in-basket items requires action.

3. Proceed to the in-basket items.

In-basket Item #1

Telephone Message

WHILE YOU WERE OUT:

TO: Dr. Smith
FROM: Elsie Mayhem, Secretary
RE: Lead article, Mr. Robert Sadler, Editor, Journal ViewPoint
        Newspaper
DATE: August 10

Since I knew you'd be getting in Monday morning, I scheduled your interview with my brother for Tuesday afternoon at 1 PM. I thought it would really be a good idea to have him do an article on you as you begin your first year as our educational leader.

In-basket Item #2

Dear Dr. Smith,

Let me be among the first to welcome you to Hill Top School. This school has been one of my fastest growing accounts, exceeding $23,000 in gross sales during its annual candy bar sale last year. Much of this growth can be attributed to your predecessor who realized what extra money could do in making opportunities available to students and staff alike.

This year's promotion kick-off has been scheduled for October 19. With some of the new prizes we have obtained, I'm sure that this campaign will be the best ever. I will be dropping by in the near future to discuss our kickoff assembly and some of the really great ideas I have for promoting your school's campaign.

I look forward to our meeting.

Sincerely,

Wes Formore, Regional Rep.

In-basket Item #3

Dear Dr. Smith,

As the new school year draws close, I want to be among the first in the community to welcome you to your new challenge. As I am sure you have heard by now, although a good-hearted person, Mr. Wells left a good deal to be desired when it came to school leadership.

My wife and I tried on numerous occasions to have our Bible study group meet during the first period for any interested student, however, Mr. Wells failed to see the value of such an inspirational time. Rather, he kept telling us that we could not use school property or school time to discuss the ramifications of today's problems as they relate to the Scriptures.

As a tax payer in this community, we request your assistance in seeing that our community's children have the opportunity to relate their problems to the Lord. We are available to meet with you and discuss a starting date and time.

Sincerely,

Rev. Billy Joe Emmanuel

In-basket Item #4

Dr. Smith--1

On behalf of the Hill Top School Booster Club, we want to welcome you to the first of many successful years with our school and community. Our booster club supports not only athletics within our school, but also academic pursuits. At the present time we are completing the purchase of a network server for the school so each classroom will have the capability to go onto the "Information Super Highway."

The primary method we have used to fund our projects has been through our annual candy sale. Last year, we grossed $23,000, however, we only realized a profit of $8,500. According to Mr. Wes Formore, the candy sale rep., the remaining money was used for promotion and prizes. We think we can do better! Our executive committee has been meeting over the summer and we have come up with ideas we need to discuss. We just think that we can do better than a 37% profit margin.

Please give me a call so we can set up a meeting to discuss our plans.

Sincerely,

Elizabeth Dwill

In-basket Item #5

TO: Dr. Smith
FROM: Elsie
RE: Speaker for Pre-planning meeting
DATE: 8/12/95, 3:15 PM

Just got a call from Jonathan Elderson. He has been rushed to the hospital with an emergency appendectomy and will not be able to keynote the Pre-Planning workshop, scheduled by Mr. Wells, on Wednesday morning. I didn't want to disturb your last weekend at home before the "rat race" begins so I waited to tell you. Perhaps you could do one of those talks that the interview committee heard you give.

In-basket Item #6

TO: All Administrators in the HT School System
FROM: Dr. Roberta Conrad, Superintendent
RE: Weekly administrative meetings
DATE: 8/10/95

As we prepare for another fantastic year at HTSS, I would like all of you to circle Tuesday mornings beginning the week of 8/16/95 at 8:30 for our weekly administrative sessions. I am asking Dr. Smith, the new principal at the Hill Top School, to serve as our host for our first meeting so we all get an opportunity to visit in the newly refurbished school. The remaining meetings for this month will rotate as before.

I look forward to seeing all of you on August 17th. Please be prepared to share your career goals for the coming year.

In-basket Item #7

Dr. Smith--

I'm sure that you have heard several stories by now about Mr. Wells and his style of leadership or lack thereof. For the past five years I have been trying to convince him that this school is getting soft on discipline...for students as well as staff. Many of the staff members leave the school during the day to "go to the bank" or "run errands." Meanwhile, those of us who remain behind are left with two classes to watch, phones to answer, or messages to take. As a teacher, I am not paid to take messages or answer the office phone; I'm paid to teach!! My classes--one at a time!!

From what we have all heard about you, the behavior which existed previously will not be tolerated. Let me say, "Thank goodness for that." I look forward to working closely with you so that we can bring some respect back to the teaching profession and to the reputation of Hill Top School.

Sincerely,

Joseph P. Whitehead, Chair
Science Department

In-basket Item #8

MEMO

TO: All building Principals
FROM: Hazel Forney, Transportation
RE: Change of Bus routes
DATE: 8/11/95

As I am sure you all know by now, the new bus schedule has been mailed to each student's home and has been printed once in the Journal ViewPoint. Pretty much, the routes are the same as last year's with one exception. The first run in the afternoon leaves the Hill Top School five minutes earlier than last year so we can be sure to have enough time to be back for the athletic practice run. This should not be any big deal since HTSS already exceeds the state minimum for education time in all of our schools by twenty-eight minutes per week.

If you have any questions, please give me a call or see me at the boss's meeting before pre-planning.

In-basket Item #9

TO: Dr. Smith
FROM: Elsie
RE: Faculty room price increase
DATE: 8/11/95

The Pepsi man just told me that with the increase in the price of Pepsi we would
have to raise the price per can in the lounge from .45 to .50. This will still leave
us with a six cents per can profit for the slush fund. Since you were not available
last week, I told him to go ahead and make the change on the machine. I hope
you agree.

In-basket Item #10

8/12/95

Dr. Smith,

I'm sorry to hit you with something like this right off the bat, but our school has consistently been short-changed within the music department. There is a tremendous amount of pressure placed on me, my staff, and the students to have a winning, eye-appealing, musical band show, however, Dr. Conrad and that lackey of an athletic director she has NEVER had our practice field lined. And since no one but God and the football team can ever get on the football field except for games, we need HELP!!

Please see what you can do about at least getting our field lined so when we go out on a Friday night we at least look like we practiced.

Thanks, and once again, sorry for hitting you with this so soon.

Jim Taylor, Band Director

P. S. Welcome to Hill Top School

In-basket Item #11

8/12/95

Dr. Smith,

I know you are extremely busy, however, I am just letting you know that all the principals get together for lunch every Wednesday at noon at Bigelow's. There are no AP's, central office types or secretaries...just the six of us. I'll stop by to pick you up at 11:30 Wednesday morning...the first lunch is on me.

Bill

In-basket Item #12

8/12/95

Dear Dr. Smith,

Let me join with other members of the school community in welcoming you to the Hill Top School. As President of the Hill Top PTO, we provide a variety of educational offerings for parents and friends of the school. In addition, we combine forces with the Booster Club in sponsoring the school's annual fund raiser.

Our first meeting for the new school year will be held on the Tuesday, August 31 at 7:30 PM in the school's newly remodeled auditorium. This meeting is generally our best attended of the year. We are inviting you to be our guest speaker. This would be a great opportunity for you to present your views on the school and to meet your students' parents. I'll give you a call the week of the 16th to see if you will accept my offer.

Best wishes for a great year.

Sincerely,

Georgiana Wellman

In-Basket II
End of the Year

Background

You are Dr. Smith, and you are completing your first year as principal of Hill Top School. It is May 20th, and you have gone to the school on a Saturday morning to check over your mail and telephone messages. You have been out of town since Wednesday evening, as the result of a family emergency.

Instructions

1.   You will be given 60 minutes to read and take action on all of the in-basket items presented following the instructions. You are not expected merely to describe what you would do, but to do it. For example, if you decide to write a letter, then compose the letter. If you decide to telephone an individual or have a conference with someone, then outline your objectives, as well as the main points or questions that you would present.

2.   Each of the in-basket items requires action.

3.   Proceed to the in-basket items.

In-basket Item #1

15 May

MEMO

TO: Dr. Smith
FROM: John Tuba

I submitted my request to conduct summer band lessons in March so that it would be placed on the board agenda at the April meeting. In reviewing the minutes from the May board meeting, I noticed that this item has still not been brought to a vote.

Everyone in the community takes great pride in the effort of our students when they see them marching at football games or parades, but the only way this caliber of musician can be maintained requires us to invest in their summer training. It seems as though someone is trying to deliberately stop this program. It is imperative that with only 20 days of school left that a decision be made so that publicity for the program can get to the students.
For the sake of our band--PLEASE HELP!!

In-basket Item #2

TELEPHONE MESSAGE:

For: Dr. Smith
From: Jim Engleman (Channel 12 Live Action News)
Time: 1:15 pm, Thursday

Please call him back ASAP. He is putting together a group of educators to face off against the Society Against Thematic Teaching (SATT) and wants you on the panel.

In-basket Item #3

12 May 1995

Dear Dr. Smith,

The little woman and I are concerned about our daughter, Sandy, and the poor performance she has turned in on her report card. We all know that girls can't possibly do as well as boys in some subjects, but, come on, she should at least be doing B work in english. What with summer coming on and all, what do you think about us getting her enrolled in a summer school program to bring up them awful grades in math and science and history.
Please get back to me so as we can make plans for our summer vacation (them fish are biting like crazy, you know). Our number is 367-9353.

Sincerely,

Johnny Bass

Feb

In-basket Item #4

Dr. Smith,

In the past, the Mr. Dorfman (*the former principal*) distributed a "Closing School" form to all the teachers. This form informed the faculty what they had to turn in, put away, etc. so the summer crew could come by and do repair work and painting. Do you have any plans to do something similar? Would you like to see what was done before? (I have some left over from last year)
Also, Mr. Dorfman developed a form for teachers to request various repair work to be done to their rooms. I also have examples of this for you if you would like to see them.
Let me know what your plans are and I will be glad to get things put together.

Herbert Helpful
Secretary

In-Basket Item #5

May 15

Dr. Smith,

Do you have any problems with my taking my classes outside? The kids in my classes get so restless this time of year.

Wilma Flowers
Spanish Teacher

In-Basket Item #6

                    May 19

Dr. Smith, I just received a call from my wife. As you know, she is in the Navy.
Well, she is being transferred to another location out-of-state. She will have to
leave in two weeks and, of course, she wants me to go with her. I really hate to
leave my job, and I would like to stay until at least the end of the school year, but
when I mentioned this to her, she didn't seem too receptive. I'm not sure what I
should do. Do you have any advice?

                                        Herbert Helpful
                                        Secretary

In-basket #7

Memorandum

To: Dr. Smith

From: Robert Squirrel, Teacher

Date: February 4, 1996

Subject: Harassment

The purpose of this memorandum is to register a formal complaint against Ms. Walker, our assistant principal. This woman has sexually harassed me on numerous occasions, and I want it to stop! She has made remarks about my butt, asked me if I sleep in the nude, and pinched me on the buttocks on several occasions. Three different times, she propositioned me. Yes, I am a new teacher, but I do not believe I should have to take this kind of abuse! Other teachers have told me that she has done similar things to them. I am concerned about my career. I need your help.

In-basket #8

MAY

Doctor SMITH

MONDAY *going* to Be A Day

YOU WILL NEVER forget

A *bomb* IS GOING to G 0

OFf THAT morning You

Better Take this Seriously

  kids.

OuT of The SCHOOL

In-Basket Item #9

May 17, 1995

Dr. Smith,

I know you are busy but I think we got a problem on our hands. Some of these kids are using smokeless tobacco in school and it is staining the floor and some of the furniture where they spit. I heard that Mr. Stikwell is using the stuff at school. I mean if teacher can use it what can we expect of the kids. Anyway, I think something's got to be done about it soon

Thanks.

Tidy Bowl.

In-Basket #10

May 17th

Dr. Smith,

I am not sure what I would do about this referral. As you probably know, Billy Bob Morris (the student) is the son of one of the school board members. I have never gotten along with the old man too well (him and me were on rival teams when we were in high school) so I would appreciate it if you would handle this one.

Hill Top School

Student Discipline Referral Form

Student's Name : <u>Billy Bob Morris</u>
Date : <u>Thursday</u>

Teacher : <u>Jack Stilwell</u>

Problem: <u>Kid keeps fooling around and is disrespectful to me. I am sick and tired of this kid and I don't want him back in class until he shapes up.</u>

In-Basket Item #11

May 18th

Dr. Smith,

For some time now, I have been wanting to bring something to your attention, but my daughter has not wanted me to contact you about the matter. However, I feel now that I must say something, whether my daughter wants me to or not.

You are probably not aware of this, but one of your teachers, a Miss Snow, is dating a high school student and from what I hear, things have progressed pretty far if you know what I mean. I think this kind of a situation sets a poor example for students, and it makes it difficult for those of us parents who are trying to set a moral tone in our own families. I know you will want to take a strong stand on this. The talk around town is that this boy already has Miss Snow in trouble if you know what I mean and that she is considering an abortion.

Obviously, Miss Snow should not be allowed to continue in her position.

Sincerely,

(Mrs.) Sally Parks

In-Basket #12

May 19th

Dear Dr. Smith.

      I would like to register formally my objection to the way my daughter has been treated in physical education class. My daughter signed-up for weight lifting training 2nd semester after the school promoted this curriculum change for girls. It has come to my attention that the new football coaches, who are now on campus replacing the present coaches and getting football players ready for spring training, have discontinued the girls' weight lifting program during 5th period, and are using the weight room with <u>football players only </u>during this time.   It appears to me that my daughter's rights have been violated and that this condition is in violation of Title IX requirements/regulations.

      I expect my daughter to be back in the weight lifting room Monday afternoon, May 22, 1995 during 5th period physical education class continuing her weight lifting training.   Because of all that is involved in this situation and the possible repercussions I will not identify myself or my daughter. However, if this matter is not addressed appropriately by Monday as requested, I am prepared to take this to the Federal Courts. THANK YOU for your cooperation.

Hill Top School
123 Top of the Hill Lane
Hill Valley, USA 33333

Dr. Smith, Principal
Ms. Walker, Assistant Principal

Appendix H

Case Studies

Case Study I - The New Principal Address

Case Study II - Two High Schools versus One High School

Case Study III - Zero Tolerance Fighting Policy

Case Study IV - The Pregnant Student Teacher

I

The New Principal Address

THE SETTING:

You have just been informed that, beginning next week, you will become the principal at the Hill Top High School, a small rural high school (grades 9-12) in the middle of the state. The community in which the school is located is comprised of people who can trace their roots to the development of the community some 150 years ago. Most of the people within the community are engaged in either agriculture (small, family-owned farms) or work in the local textile mill which has been experiencing cut-backs in recent years due to the importation of goods from overseas. The board is comprised of three men and two women, one of whom claims that she alone was responsible for hiring the new superintendent. This person's husband was president of the Hill Top Sports Boosters prior to the hiring of the new superintendent.

The superintendent of the system is in her second year of a three year contract. She was brought in from outside the system amidst a scandal involving receipts from football and basketball games. In her second year, she found that the scandal directly involved the high school principal as well and she moved to remove him. Following a lengthy legal battle, the principal plea bargained to step down as principal provided he could remain as the driver education teacher for the school. As the driver education teacher, he has been instrumental in keeping "the air stirred-up" for the assistant principal who served as the interim principal. Although this person was in the running for the position to which you have just been appointed, the superintendent thought it would be best to bring in "...some new blood to get the school going again."

Faculty and students have been feeling the effects generated by the problems with the high school principal. Members of the high school faculty have expressed concern about the looseness of the student discipline as the assistant has tried to be everyone's friend; students and faculty alike. Faculty members have begun "cracking down" on the students to restore the lacking discipline which led to open student rebellion two weeks ago with the students walking out of their classes at 11:30AM in protest to the mistreatment they are feeling. In addition the faculty has been ignoring the requests of the acting principal saying that they want to be involved in the decision-making process and that they are too busy trying to keep the students in line that they do not have the time to get what they term "busy work" reports completed.

THE PROBLEM:

The superintendent will introduce you to the faculty and students at an all-school assembly on Monday morning. Your assignment is to use the information gained on organizational thought, school climate, pupil control ideology, and morale-building/decision-making and develop the address you will present which will, in fact, set the tone of your administrative tenure.

II

Two High Schools vs. One High School

The Community:

Hill Top County is located in the rural South. Residents of Hill Top number approximately 35,000 represented by a 40% minority of African American and Hispanics, and 60% white population. The community is progressive in its support of education and the recruiting of new business and industrial prospects. The community contains a popular 2 year Junior college, an agricultural experiment station, numerous corporate agricultural research facilities, and a living history museum. The Hill Top County community was selected as one of the 100 best communities in the United States in which to live.

The School System:

Hill Top schools has an enrollment of approximately 7,800 students. These students attended the following school organizational pattern:

  5 - Pre-K through 4th grade schools
  1 - Pre-K through 7th grade school
  2 - 5th through 7th grade Middle schools
  1 - 8th through 9th grade Junior High School
  1 - 10th through 12th grade High School.

The buildings are well maintained and attractive. To accommodate the increase in student population over the years, new media centers, additional constructed classrooms, and portable classrooms were added to several schools.

The local community has been a proponent of a strong educational system often giving potential business and industrial customers, interested in re-locating, tours of the schools as a selling point. Curriculum and instructional technologies are current and progressive. Community support and lottery dollars have placed many computers and computer labs in the schools. Each elementary classroom has a minimum of 3 networked computers attached to a file server that contains a curriculum for math and reading. All schools have satellite dishes, modems for the internet, and the high school utilizes the Channel 1 technology. The school system and employees have been a unified and stable institution and a point of pride in the community.

The Problem:

The Hill Top community has been a fortunate and prosperous community. The location of the community at the crossroads of important transportation routes for the south has attracted several major industries resulting in a steady increase in population. This continuous increase in the school age population has begun placing requirements on the school system that the present school structures are having difficulties accommodating. Anticipating a growth rate that in the near future would place a severe burden on the present school buildings, the Board of Education adopted a plan of action.

The Board of Education, with the assistance of individuals, community groups, and civic organizations, appointed a diverse group of 35 members from the community, the Board of Education, and the schools as a study commission. This study commission was given the charge to study the school system and make recommendations to the school board. The study commission availed themselves to research and experts in the areas of school organization, curriculum, buildings, financial concerns, and growth patterns in formulating their recommendations. Following more than a year long active and very involved process, the commission made its recommendations to the school board. The commission recommended the following school organization and building plan:

- 4 -   Pre-K through 2nd grade schools
- 1 -   Pre-K through 5th grade school
- 3 -   3rd - 5th grade schools (schools converted from 1 former Pre-K through 4th grade school and the 2 former middle schools)
- 2 -   6th - 8th grade Middle Schools (**The construction of 1 new Middle School** and the renovation of the Jr. High School as a Middle School)
- 2 -   9th - 12th grade High Schools (**The construction of 1 new High School** and the renovation of the present High School)

These recommendations were designed to take advantage of the maximum capital outlay funds available from the state, develop a more common grade level organization to maximize use of instructional resources, form 2 true Middle Schools, and place the 9th grade at the High Schools were they are traditionally located.

The commission had the choice of recommending the building of 1 large or 2 smaller High Schools. One large High School containing the grades of 9th through 12th with the present population would number approximately 2100 students. Growth predictions would place this number around 2500 in a few years and close to 3000 in 10 to 15 years. After researching the advantages and disadvantages of the large High School verses the small High School and construction costs, the commission recommended the construction of the 2 smaller High Schools (2 High Schools containing 1000+ students each are not small High Schools).

The Board of Education, after studying the recommendations of the commission, voted unanimously to accept the plan. The Board began immediately writing the facilities plan to meet the state's requirements and developing a bond referendum plan for funding. In the first few days and weeks after the board's acceptance, proceedings progressed smoothly. As the realization that the traditions of a 1 High School community were coming to an end, an uneasiness began to develop in the community.

Individuals in the community began to speak out against the 2 High School concept. As plans were developed and implemented for the bond referendum, individual concerns developed into group concerns. The concerns voiced in the community included the idea that one High School would be for the rich students and one for the minority students, taxes would be raised at such a level that it would be a burden on the farmers, elderly community members, and the average tax payer. The cost of operating 2 High Schools, how they would be staffed and the curriculum offerings were brought into question. Much concern was given to the fact that the sports teams, especially football, band and other school activities, would drop down in classification from what many consider the most prominent region and classification in the nation.

As the promotion of the bond referendum was introduced, formal opposition to the plan was organized. The Concerned Citizens Group began organizational meetings, advertizing in the local media, and challenged the School Board on every issue. The School Board was accused of giving false and misleading information on taxes and funding requirements. School officials and administrators were accused of forcing the School Boards ideas upon teachers during faculty meetings, and promoting the bond referendum during school hours with students as well as using school resources in promotional activities.

As the bond referendum approached, the opposition increased their pressure to defeat the Board's plan. Critical advertisements and letters appeared in the media attacking the School Board, the Superintendent, Individual school administrators, teachers and community members supporting the plan. The School Board and the Concerned Citizens group each held conferences on the local television and radio stations promoting their cause.

As the pressure mounted, divisions began to occur in the rank and file of the school employees. Many teachers as well as non-certified employees began to voice opposition to the School Board's plan and some openly demonstrated support for the opposition. The Athletic Director and Head football coach went on a regional television newscast and voiced his opposition to the Board's 2 High School plan and in support of current athletic competition. This was followed two days later with a front page story in the local newspaper where he again voiced his opposition to the Board's 2 High School Plan in support of current athletic competition.

The quiet, peaceful, harmonious community of Hill Top had become anything but what it once was. Personal attacks on individual's character and mistrust of neighbors became the rule of the day. Divisions became so great that shopping, business, and social habits changed based on the position individuals supported. When the voters went to the polls, they rejected the referendum's request for funding for the school improvement projects.

Questions to Begin Discussion:

1.   When the Board of Education formulates a facilities plan for the school district, should this plan be supported by the employees of the Board?

2.   What is the role of 1st amendment rights of employees in this situation?

3.   What is your position of teachers going public with their disagreements with the Board of Education?

4.   What is your position on the Athletic Director and Head football coach going public in the media to express his opposition to his employer.

5.   Do public school employees have an implied duty to support the decisions and policies of their Boards of Education?

6.   What does the research indicate about school size and effectiveness?

7.   What is your position on advantages/disadvantages of one large High School vs. two small High Schools?

8.   What are the advantages/disadvantages of the 9th grade contained in a Middle/Jr. High School vs. a High School?

III

Zero Tolerance Fighting Policy

The Policy:

Hill Top County Schools has not been spared the severe discipline problems gripping other school systems nation wide. Board of Education members, sensing the increasing concerns from the community and educators over the frequency and severity of discipline problems, passed a Zero Tolerance Fighting Policy. The Board of Education, in passing this policy, emphasized that all students had a right to a safe and secure school environment conducive to learning. In addition to this policy, security officers were placed in the High School and Junior High School.

The Board of Education specified that the Zero Tolerance Policy would apply only to students in the Middle Schools, the Junior High and the High School. The policy stated that in the event a fight occurred, the appropriate law enforcement officers would be called and each student involved in the fight would be placed under arrest with no exceptions. The policy would be applied equally to all students in all situations.

The Problem:

The Zero Tolerance Policy has been in effect for approximately two years without any noticeable problems. Several fights have occurred and these students were escorted away by law enforcement personnel. As a result of the policy and security officers in the buildings, fighting in the schools has decreased significantly. This year, there has been an unusual number of fights occurring especially in the Middle Schools (Grades 5, 6, & 7). On several occasions, very young students from the Middle Schools, especially minority students, were involved in fights and were placed under arrest by law enforcement officers in accordance with Board Policy. Prior to enacting this Policy, discipline and order in the Middle Schools had been a primary concern of school officials and the Board of Education. Following policy enactment, discipline and order continued to be a concern at the Middle Schools.

At the October Board of Education the Rev. J. D. Faith requested and was granted an opportunity to address the Board. The Rev. Faith implored the Board to rescind the Zero Tolerance policy because young boys and girls were being taken to jail, the policy was not being implemented fairly, and the school administrators were not consistent in calling law enforcement officers. The Board indicated that they would look into how the policy was being enforced, but had not intentions of rescinding the policy.

The following day, the front page of the local newspaper carried an article and interview with the Rev. Faith. He charged, in the paper, that decisions to call law enforcement officials was based on race, that young children were being thrown in jail with criminals, and that the real criminals were the school officials. He suggested that they were the ones that should be thrown in jail for terrible injustice they were inflicting upon the young people of the community. The Rev. Faith promised that the fight had just begun and that he would not rest until this unjust policy was removed from the school system.

Possible Discussion Questions:

1. What is your position on the use of a Zero Tolerance Fighting Policy?

2. Do you believe a Zero Tolerance Fighting Policy is an effective deterrent in schools?

3. If you are in favor of a Zero Tolerance Policy, what grade levels do you believe this policy should include?

4. What is your position on the use of law enforcement officers in the Zero Tolerance Fighting Policy? What options would/would you not recommend?

5. Following the charges and concerns leveled by the Rev. Faith, the Superintendent has informed each school administrator to prepare a response concerning the Policy. What will your response be?

IV

The Pregnant Student Teacher

The Student Teacher. Mary Filmore was a popular college student. As a freshman, Mary was the starting center for the womens basketball team. Mary rapidly became a very popular girl on campus and attended many social functions. Participation in these social functions led a serious romance with another student which resulting in the birth of a daughter. Mary left school for one quarter and then returned to complete her basketball career as well as to obtain her teaching degree.

THE SCHOOL. Hill Top Elementary School is a moderately to large elementary school of approximately 600 students. This is a neighborhood school with more students walking and riding in family cars to school than riding the bus. The school community is 90% white middle class, with 7% black and 3% Hispanic students.

THE PROBLEM. Mary Filmore had completed her course requirements and was now ready for her student teaching assignment. The college, along with the school district personnel director, assigned Mary Filmore to do her student teaching in second grade at the Hill Top Elementary School. Mary appeared to settle into the student teaching role without too much difficult. The students liked her and she was very sociable with the faculty and staff of the School.

Within a couple of weeks, the principal detected a rumor that Mary Filmore was pregnant. He was told that he should observe Ms. Filmore more closely because the evidence was showing. Following a casual observation, the principal determined that this was indeed the case. It was determined that Ms. Filmore had been pregnant for some time, and that the wearing of loose fitting clothing had disguised the condition well.

After making several inquires in many different places the principal determined several facts about he situation. It was found that Ms. Filmore would be delivering this baby within three weeks of completing her student teaching - if the days had been counted correctly. It was also determined that Ms. Filmore was not married, and that this was her second illegitimate child.

As the year progressed and Ms. Filmore's condition became obvious to everyone, concerns began to surface about Ms. Filmore. Teachers in the building as well as parents began expressing concerns about the values, ethics, and especially moral character of Ms. Filmore. Some teachers and parents finally expressed to the principal that they felt this was the wrong message to be sending to students, and that Ms. Filmore should resign her student teaching duties. Since the Superintendent is now aware of this situation, he has asked you to make a full report to him on Monday. You have called a meeting with the University Personnel to discuss this matter, and will be consulting with the Superintendent following this meeting.

Possible Discussion Questions

1.   Should the University (if they had known) informed the School System that an unmarried pregnant student teacher will be attending?

2.   Should the school and master teacher be aware of the condition of incoming student teachers?

3.   Are there moral issues involved here that take precedence over individual rights?

4.   Should the student teacher have elected on her own not to attend school during this time?

5.   What should the principal tell the staff and faculty about this applicant?

Appendix I

The Leadership Portfolio

THE LEADERSHIP PORTFOLIO NARRATIVE WORKSHEET

This worksheet has been designed to help you get started on the important narrative section of your leadership portfolio. Please, describe your accomplishments and give examples, where appropriate, to further illustrate your responses.

1.   Describe your past teaching responsibilities.

2.   Describe your teaching methods and explain <u>why</u> you teach as you do. (Particular attention should be given to strategy and implementation.) Give examples.

3.   Describe course projects, class assignments or other activities that have helped you integrate your subject matter with your students' outside experiences.

4.   Describe any administrative responsibilities.

5.   Describe techniques you use in school leadership and explain why you lead in this particular manner. Give examples.

6.   Describe specific leadership activities that help you relate to certified and non-certified personnel, students, and parents.

7.   If you overheard teachers talking about you and your leadership style in the teacher's lounge, what would they likely be saying? What would you like them to say? Why is that important to you?

8.   If you overhead students talking about you and your leadership style in the cafeteria, what would they likely be saying? What would you like them to say? Why is that important to you?

9.   Give examples and describe specific ways that you motivate certified and non-certified employees to help them achieve better performance.

10.   Give examples and describe specific ways that you motivate students to help them achieve better performance.

11.   Describe your efforts to develop your leadership effectiveness.

    a.)   **Workshops/Conferences Attended**.

    b.)   **Informal assessment of your own leadership style.**

    c.)   **Describe your presentations and/or publications on teaching and/or administration.**

12.   How do you stay current in leadership? How do you translate this new knowledge into your leadership activities?

PRIMARY LEVEL
ADMINISTRATIVE PORTFOLIO NARRATIVE

Table of Contents

Narrative

Appendices

Leadership Philosophy

An effective administrator is one who shares decision making with the faculty when the opportunity arises. She is also the administrator which can be seen and heard. I personally appreciate administrators who visit my classroom and hold individual conferences with me where both positive and constructive negative statements are made about my abilities.

First, I do not ask employees to do anything I would not do myself. I do take time to hear the suggestions of others and to always say thank-you for duties completed with a sincere smile on my face. All people in my eyes are equal. I make it a point to make each employee feel needed, because they are. A school is a tight knit family, all employees are like the spokes in a wheel. If we do not function together we break down and get nowhere.

In addition, I lead as I like to be led, in a non-authoritarian manner. For example, I like for teachers to believe I act as an overseer as opposed to a dictator. I like to talk through problems and guide employees to making the right decisions as opposed to demanding staff to do certain things or make certain changes. This allows an employee to positively grow. Praise is a big plus in any administrator. I do my best to praise a lot whether the accomplishment is large or small. One thing I do is send employees Happy Grams (written notes of praise). Copies of Happy Grams can be found under Happy Gram in Appendix B. Also, when a large project is to be accomplished, such as organization of an yearly project, I like to plan in small segments. A copy of projects, in which I planned in small segments is found under Olympics in Appendix A and Student Assistance Program, S.T.P., in Appendix H.

I also believe in an open door policy. If I have a problem or a concern, I like knowing I can go to a person and have my concern heard, and I extend the same courtesy to all people I am involved with at the professional level. I have found that one of the best ways to be effective is to always wear a smile and have a positive attitude. After all, happiness is contagious.

An effective administrator is one who has focus. The focus in my eyes is the mission and vision of a school. All decisions should be made in the best interest of children as reflected in a mission and a vision I wrote while I enrolled in a personnel class. (A copy of the mission and vision is found under Scheduling in Appendix G).

According to my philosophy, the community would need to be used as connectors to the real world. The community will need to be utilized as career consultants, leaders, and educators. In my own words, a community not involved is an education lost. Students should be exposed to the community and community members should have an open door policy into the school with the understanding that learning and the sharing of knowledge are the two prominent reasons foe entering a school.

In conclusion, all the bodies are important. Whether a body is certified, non-certified, parent, community member, or student, a school could not function with one and not the other. Praise is owed to all, so growth within the setting can continue.

Teaching and Learning Philosophy

First, I fully believe that class size should be kept at a maximum of 20, regardless of student age. To fully implement a hands-on, student centered curricula class size has to be low in number. For individual student attention to occur as often as it should, class size also has to be kept at a maximum of 20. Students benefit more from a small class size than they do from the addition of a paraprofessional.

As an early childhood teacher, I believe that children learn best when exposed to a variety of teaching methods. Since no two children learn the same way, I implement a variety of teaching methods in my instruction. By using a variety of techniques, the needs of all students are met. I have housed within this portfolio outlines of teaching methods I use in my classroom (see Teaching Strategies under Appendix L).

Ideal classroom organization would focus attention in the center of the classroom placing emphasis on the student. Noise level, as long as it is productive noise, is not to be heavily controlled. The classroom needs to have sinks, labs, and space available for all necessary equipment and materials for student-centered activities. Students, in this type of free-flow classroom, would be able to "feel" the freedom in the classroom and therefore take advantage of the freedom which would lead to student-engaged learning. To take from Mathematics Their Way, learning by doing is remembered. I have taken several workshops which focus around integrating subject areas and hands-on experiences (see Workshops Appendix L).

In addition to using a variety of teaching techniques, I believe that in order to receive the most from a student, praise is a must. I am constantly praising students regardless of the accomplishment. However, at the same time students in my room know that if a rule is broken there is a consequence. Time-out is often utilized in my room. (One approach I use is S.O.S., a parenting technique, for a copy of this technique see S.O.S. under Appendix E).

As an educator, I believe that I need to have realistic expectations for each child and expect those expectations from each child. Verbally, I announce to children what I expect of them. My reasoning is that this allows children to know that I care for them and their learning. In addition, I believe in the philosophy that what you expect from children is probably what you will get; a self-fulfilling prophecy. If a child falls short of meeting required criteria, then it is my responsibility to refer the child to Student Support Team (S.S.T. see Appendix H).

As a future parent, I would want to be kept abreast of my child's progress. I believe in numerical symbolism as well as informal verbal evaluation. I am in favor of a report card along with portfolio assessment. This method allows for both grades and eye-to- eye contact between the teacher and the parents.

Through Early Childhood courses that I have taken in the past, I have seen how important it is to focus around themes which include knowledge in a child's life surroundings. For example, at the kindergarten level the theme of farm is taught because, in the rural community where I teach, farming plays a big role in terms of economics. The culminating activity for this unit, is to visit a farm. At times it is difficult to visit an outside source, so the source is brought to the school as noted in Visitors under (see Appendix E).

My philosophy of education involves experienced learning with individual summation. Learning with a purpose and a re-addressing of experiences will only reinforce learning and serve as a stepping stone for future learning. As a teacher, one can only hope for and should always accept student diversity. The word human itself implies, in my opinion, difference.

In conclusion, as a teacher, I do my best to bring the outside world into the classroom through hands-on experiences with realistic materials, by integrating subject areas in such a way that the subject area is viewed by the students as relevant. In addition, I praise students appropriately and have rules and consequences understood by both students and parents.

Administrative Responsibilities

I have had the benefit of being responsible for numerous administrative responsibilities. Among those responsibilities are duties such as lunch, hall, office, and bus. A part of these duties included a meeting with parapros which resulted from an observation in the lunchroom. During the meeting, I praised the parapros several times as well as encouraged them to walk while on duty. I also encouraged them to help in seeing that the lunchroom is kept clean. Due to the fact that the school could be held liable for any injuries that could occur as a result of an unsafe lunchroom, I did a follow-up on the lunchroom to observe, if in fact, the parapros understood and obeyed my instructions. (An agenda for this meeting can be found under parapro in Appendix B).

Office duties included dispensing medication, calling parents, writing tardy slips, answering the phone, and relaying messages to teachers. This experience allowed me to have both a larger appreciation for secretaries and administrators. Time spent in the office also gave me the opportunity to observe numerous parent conferences conducted by both the principal and assistant principal. I was also allowed to independently handle discipline problems (see Discipline, Appendix E).

I have spent several hours managing by walking around. During this time, I was making myself available for anyone who may need assistance. This time also gave me the opportunity to examine the facilities for possible hazards, as well as, safe conditions which would allow me to praise custodians.

During the 1994-95 school year, I have been responsible for chairing an Olympic Committee. In this position, I invited "Izzy," the Olympic Mascot, to our school. As a result of "Izzy's" visit, I was interviewed by a local television station and appeared on the eleven o'clock news. Upon leaving the building, "Izzy" and her companion informed me that the program I planned was wonderful and that the school would receive a rating of excellent from the Olympic Youth Committee. Other events , which occurred as a result of this committee are monthly programs hosted by each grade level, an Olympic Open House, and an Olympian speaker. (A copy of bulletins, agendas, and other paperwork are found in Appendix A).

Analysis and Description of Leadership Techniques, Strategies

Adults are like children in the sense that praise causes them to excel and work harder. Praise is a powerful motivator. Both adults and children like to know what is expected of them.

I have found that to be an effective administrator, I must be able to work effectively with all people who are involved in the school. These groups of people being certified staff, non-certified staff, students and parents. While taking Clinical Supervision, I was asked by the professor to role play various situations involving certified personnel. This project exposed me to various ways of approaching the same situation. The techniques used in the class can be applied to non-certified staff as well as to parents and students. For example, I role played a situation in which I was an administrator dealing with an educator who had received numerous rates of "needs improvements." This type of situation, where I am asked to handle a delicate situation could arise with a student, a parent, or non-certified employee.

In addition to writing a vision and a mission, I had the opportunity of being asked to create a staffing project as a requirement. Included in the personnel project were: lunch schedule, exploratory schedule, number of teachers needed on the staff, as well as other components. The complete project can be found under Appendix G.

The school of my dreams, would have interior walls full of children's creations. By creations I do not mean patterns created by teachers; I mean art and writings which reflect student thought. The thought of a child or a young adult would jump out at a visitor.

Due to the current state of affairs, I would insist, as a future administrator, that all visitors check-in at the office; however, after signing-in I would not limit visitors to staying at the office. I would allow visitors to go to rooms to show them that I encourage community involvement. I would want the size, shape, and coloration of the rooms to promote direct attention to the student. The grounds of a school should, if land is available, have a workable garden, forestry department, and nature trail regardless of grade level. Everything at a school should exemplify student-centered work not teacher-centered.

In conclusion, I would hope that all staff would view me as an organized, hardworking, non-authoritarian figure, who is capable of seeing a project from beginning to end. This is extremely important to me because I do not want to be viewed as "bossy," I want people to feel as though they could share anything with me, without feeling threatened. In jobs where "bossy" people are the boss, morale is usually low. This I want to avoid.

Assessment of Effectiveness

In each position I have held, I have received all "S's" on G.T.O.I. evaluations. My principal recorded on yearly evaluations that I promote learning in my classroom by being positive. Copies of my evaluation are housed under G.T.O.I. in Appendix B. Fellow staff and students have acknowledged my behaviors through notes and cards for examples of correspondence see information From Others under Appendix K.

Awards and Recognition

I have been recognized for completing S.T.A.R.S. in-service and Student Assistance Program in-service. Both programs are devised to help in counseling children with drug related problems. Both programs include pulling students from classes and involving them in groups focusing on a theme such as family changes, drug and alcohol problems, school survival, and anger control.

Improvement Activities

I have attended numerous workshops during my teaching career which have enhanced me professionally. Because I have been enrolled in college courses virtually all of the years I have been teaching, lack of time has prohibited me from attending more conferences and workshops.

However, the college courses I have completed have benefitted me both professionally an personally.

By chairing the Olympic and Student Assistance Program committees, I worked with the entire staff. This impacted my leadership style tremendously. By delegating authority and a great deal of self-effort, I was able to form cohesiveness throughout the whole school. I communicated with the staff through meetings and bulletins. The projects were huge success, and I left with the impression that I was respected by the staff.

As all educators know, a career in education can be stressful. While I was enrolled in the Principles of Administration course, I was asked to give a presentation on stress. I reflect on this project for coping with stress when "one of those days" occurs. A copy of this project can be found under Stress in Appendix B.

While I enrolled in the internship, I averaged 23 hours of administrative and supervision duties each week. In addition, to this weekly time, I shadowed another administrator in a neighboring county. This allowed me to compare leadership styles.

Future Leadership Goals/Directions

My first goal is to obtain a position as an assistant principal at the elementary level. I am capable of this position, in part, due to the fact that I have worked in this area a number of years. I understand the importance of a good first start in school administration as reflected in my vision (see Appendix G) My long term goal is to be a principal. I plan on holding an assistant principalship for at least three years and then I plan on moving into the principalship.

I feel as though the mission I wrote sums-up my entire beliefs. The mission is as follows: The mission of the school is to ensure that every child lives with a positive self-concept; that we graciously give to each precious being the ability to think independently; that these students we are asked to influence are shown by example, what it means to work cooperatively in a non-threatening atmosphere.

Through example, teamwork, and student self-fulfillment, each child will achieve success. The entire staff will provide an enthusiastic, positive atmosphere which will influence the children daily. By utilizing a hands-on exploratory approach to teaching, students, through time, will gain independent thinking skills.

Elementary School
Leadership Portfolio

Narrative

Leadership Philosophy
Teaching and Learning Philosophy
Administrative Responsibilities
Analysis of Leadership Techniques, Strategies
Description of Leadership Practices
Assessment of Effectiveness
Awards and Recognition
Improvement Activities
Future Leadership Goals/ Directions
Appendices
  A   Principles of Instructional Leadership
  B   Principles of Human Resources Management
  C   Principles of Physical Resources management
  D   Principles of Fiscal Resources Management
  E   Principles of Student Personnel Management
  F   Principles of Public Relations
  G   Principles of Organization
  H   Principles of School Law and Agency
  I   Principles of Human Relations and Group Dynamics

Leadership Philosophy

Leadership is a process of giving meaningful direction to mutual effort, and causing willing effort to be given to accomplish purpose. It is a social influence process where intentional influence is exerted by one person over other people to structure the activities and relationships in a group or organization. I believe leadership is a group role where the leader can exert real leadership through effective participation in groups. The leader depends upon the frequency of interaction with the followers. As a leader, I must conceptualize tasks and communicate the approach to those tasks to others in the organization. The pattern of task identification and response forms the basis of an operating theory.

I feel the leader often deals with tasks that are not permanent solutions to needs. In such cases, the way in which people,   resources, and ideas are organized is the responsibility of the leader. The leader must be capable of structuring the organization and work environment that can respond to those needs. I think working with a diverse group of individuals with different needs and perceptions, the leader must set standards and other expectations that will affect the resolution of problems. These standards may include work habits, communication procedures, time limitations, or a host of related planning areas.

My feeling is that persons assigned to leadership positions generally must structure organizations by suggesting changes and initiating policies. One important task for a leader is using such authority to establish a desirable work climate. Such a climate is made up of the collective perceptions of persons affected by the structure of the organization Leadership is a product of human exchanges or transactions within the organization. It is essential that interpersonal relationships contribute to the attainment of desired ends. The way in which a leader interacts with others in the organization can assist in interpersonal relationships.

Teaching and Learning Philosophy

Teaching requires that the individual providing instruction have knowledge and information that the learner does not have and that the teacher have specialized skill necessary to impart that important information to the learners. The methodology varies based on the composition or learning styles of the class and the objectives of the content. A good teacher must accomplish many tasks at the same time. One such task is leadership through classroom management and organization. This is a crucial function that must be carried out daily during every aspect of the instructional process.

Another task includes preparation for instruction that requires such things as the completion of lesson plans for students. This plans provide a guide for leading the students where the teacher would have them go in learning. One other example is the frequency in assessing student progress. This provides much needed feed back in insuring that students who need remediation receive it and those who do not are able to move on.

It is important for educators to understand how students learn. This provides the basis for decisions made to provide the best possible instruction. The knowledge gained by the study of processing information makes teachers aware that for students to learn, one must have their attention. If the information provided is not received by the sensory receptors, it can not become a part of the learner's short term memory. Such information may be provided, but is lost to the student.

Maintaining the interest of the child helps to insure that students commit the material to their short term memory. Having accomplished this, the instructor can then provide the activities necessary for practice. These activities allow students to add this information to their memory. Information then becomes available for use whenever the student needs it.

I think each learner should be allowed an educational opportunity that gives them a chance to reach their potential. Since the school exists for the learner, every effort must be made   to insure adequate instruction for every child who enters the doors of the institution. The learner is a unique, free choosing, and responsible individual made up of intellect and emotion. Education allows for the needs of man when it inculcates the child with certain essential skills and knowledge which all men should possess.

Administrative Responsibilities

I have performed a number of administrative duties while employed by the county school system. The duty that I am best known for is that of school reporter for the system newsletter. It is my responsibility to gather newsworthy information at the school and compile it for the monthly publication (see Appendix F). This task requires me to keep abreast of the occurrences throughout the school. The items reported include all employees and students. With this responsibilities the task of obtaining releases for all individuals photographed that are to appear in the publication.

Another task that I perform is in the area of emergency preparedness. As coordinator of the Emergency Management Team for the elementary school, I am charged with the duty of modifying and updating the emergency plan for the school yearly (see Appendix D) . I also provide in-service training during pre-planning each year as mandated by the state regarding the emergency plan (see Appendix H) This responsibility requires that I serve on the school system's Emergency Management Team. The system team deals with the issue of management for all the schools in the county. As a member, I was involved in the implementation of the plan for the entire system (see Appendix D). Other duties performed include regular inspections of the facilities, radiological monitoring, preparing school level exercises, and keeping current evacuation plans.

A fulfilling task that I perform yearly is the campaign for the non-profit organizations in our community. As a school system member of the Organized Volunteer Effort, my responsibility is to collect money for the American Cancer Society, The American Heart Association, and The United Way (see Appendix B). In performing this task, I acquaint the employees with the program during a faculty meeting and pass out information. Then, over the next two week period, I go to each individual and collect their contributions. I find that by seeing each person in this way, it adds a personal aspect to collecting . After all contributions are made I complete the school contribution forms. I then compile and balance totals, turning them in to be used as a part of the system totals.

Serving as Community relations Coordinator for the elementary school, one task I perform involves submitting the honor roll for publication in the local newspaper (see Appendix F). This requires obtaining from teachers the names of third, fourth, and fifth grade students making the honor roll. After receiving a list for each grade level, I alphabetize them and prepare them for copy. They are then delivered for publication. At the conclusion of each year, I compile a list of students achieving honor roll for the year to be recognized during Honor's Day by the Parent Teacher's Organization.

Star Lab provided yet another opportunity for me to perform administrative tasks (see Appendix G). I am charged with obtaining dates for the lab to be used at the school. I am also required to arrange for the unit after it arrives. Once there, students in all grades must have access to it. I am responsible for organizing a schedule to be used for this purpose. The materials necessary for instructions accompanying the labs are then evaluated as well as the equipment. In addition I make several lesson presentations. At the conclusion of time allocated for use at the school my tasks involves disassembly and preparation for pick-up.

Analysis of Leadership Techniques, Strategies

The techniques I have used in school leadership have currently been limited to Influence Tactics. The primary reason is that there is no chance at all to use the Power Approach. I am not in a position to employ this approach since I am not in an administrative position. There is no threat of any act that I can use to require individuals to perform tasks.

A behavior tactic I have employed often is Rational Persuasion. In coordinating the drive to collect contributions for charitable organizations, I've had to use logical arguments to support the reasons employees should contribute. This helps to make the request viable and usually results in receiving desired contributions.

Personal Appeal is a tactic frequently used as well. In performing tasks it is sometimes necessary to appeal to feelings of loyalty and friendship toward me when requesting something. An example would be in requesting volunteers to serve at the local mall during the Education Fair (see Appendix F). When asked those who feel close to me will ultimately be the first to offer assistance because they are likely to hope for my success.

Description of Leadership Practices

In my very limited capacity as a leader, there are a few practices that I feel are worthy of applying at this stage of my development. First, as a leader, it is helpful to know who is in your charge. This knowledge is helpful in providing the basis for establishing expectations. I would never ask any employee to perform aa task that I myself would not be willing to do. Secondly, I have a need to understand fully the situation I'm involved in. Before influencing a situation, it is important for me to make certain the change will be positive. Considering all possible ramifications is important to me. Next, I feel that flexibility is necessary. My ability to adjust to the situation is one of my finest qualities. Finally, I feel that the ability to communicate is crucial. If one has vision and cannot communicate it, no true vision exists.

Assessment of Effectiveness

I feel that leader effectiveness is the extent to which the leader's organizational unit performs its task successfully and attains its goal. The attitude of the followers toward the leader is a common indicator of leader effectiveness. Objective measures of behavior, such as absenteeism, voluntary turnover, grievances, complaints to higher management, requests for transfer, and work slowdowns serve as indirect indicators of follower dissatisfaction. They may even indicate hostility toward the leader. I believe the leader's contribution to the quality of group process can be used to assess leader effectiveness also.

Awards and Recognition

In my professional career, I have been the recipient of several awards. In 1986, I was named Teacher of the Year for Pine Grove Elementary School. (See Appendix M) 1991 marks the year I received the Honor's Day award for faculty recognition. (See Appendix M) In January of 1995, I received recognition by the Lowndes County Board of Education for being selected Employee of the Month for January. (See Appendix M)

Improvement Activities

The elementary school were I am employed has in place two programs designed to foster appropriate behavior in the school environment. The first is the T.A.P. (Think! Act Positively) program. This program rewards students for appropriate behavior. Each student is assigned a team based on the colors of the rainbow. The members of that team earn tokens based on application of proper behavior. Each time an employee notices a child displaying proper behavior, the student receives a token. The behavior can range from helping a peer by picking up a book that was dropped to walking away to avoid a fight. At the end of the six week period, the team with the greatest amount of tokens wins a T.A.P. party. Students displaying improper behavior receive T.A.P. slips. Three slips during the course of any week results in assignment to T.A.P. class.   This class is for after school detention. Children are required to reflect on the inappropriate behavior they have displayed.

The second program involves peer mediation (see Appendix E). Conflict Managers are trained in the art of helping their peers resolve their differences in a positive way. When disputes arise, students can chose to have a mediator work with them to solve the problem. Those choosing to have the matter settled by the teacher still have that option.

Our school improvement activities were centered around the selection and training of these Conflict Managers. The first task involved identifying potential candidates for the 1995-1996 school year. This was accomplished by first explaining the program to the fourth grade students. Then, based on the criteria, having them vote for three people in their class that they felt would do a good job. After all students had voted, we determined winners from each class and listed them as potential managers. The next step involved conferring with their teachers to determine whether they felt favorable concerning the selection. If the teacher confirmed we accepted that student as a manager.

Notification was then given to parents with a request for permission for their child to participate. Obtaining this permission form the parents, we then scheduled training sessions for students (see Appendix E).   Once the sessions were completed we assigned future managers to current managers to allow them to observe the strategy . In addition to training, we assessed the effectiveness of the program. Researching the topic, we found an instrument we could use to evaluate the program. We reproduced the instrument and provided students and teachers a chance to respond to items relate to their feelings about the program. There was also an instrument to be completed by the managers (see Appendix E).

Future Administrative Goals/Directions

My immediate goals are to seek employment in the area of leadership and meet the requirements for enrollment in the six year program at State University. I hope to ascend to role of principal and my desire is to make a difference in the lives of children. It is my hope that I can use the information available on effective schools to create that environment in my school.

Middle School
Leadership Portfolio

TABLE OF CONTENTS

LEADERSHIP PHILOSOPHY

I have adopted the MBWA leadership style - management by walking around. I do not want of spend all my time in an office taking care of paper work. I want to be visible , available , encouraging, and enthusiastic. I want to lead by example, and I want people to follow and respect me not because of my position but because of my example and integrity.

I think dependability, responsibility, and consistency are very important qualities in a leader. I want people to know I can be depended upon to follow through with my plans or my assistance. I want to be seen as a resource for problem solving. I believe in site based management, teacher empowerment, collaboration, and peer evaluation.

TEACHING AND LEARNING PHILOSOPHY

I believe every individual has a right to an education. All students can learn and education should be student-centered. As an educator it is my responsibility to help students learn. This includes more than just being able to adequately demonstrate or verbally illustrate certain classroom skills. I want to understand the level of development of my students and be able to respond and motivate these students. An educator should be a leader with a sense of organization and projection to reach certain goals while at the same time having a sense of concern, compassion, and timing to deal with persons individually and collectively.

Education benefits not only individuals but also our entire society. The more students learn and the more students graduate from high school, the more productive members of society there will be. I enjoy being a part of this educational process.

ADMINISTRATIVE RESPONSIBILITIES

I have had administrative responsibilities as the choral director, assistant band director , CIS (Community in Schools) teacher, swim team coach, teacher support specialist, and off-campus instructor for Brewton-Parker College. Being involved in a public school music program usually involves scheduling for extra rehearsals, arranging transportation for performances, raising money through fund raisers, developing and managing the music budget, maintaining public relations through the media and public performances, keeping records, maintaining expensive musical instruments and equipment, ordering music and maintaining the music library, taking care of uniforms, and dealing with many personality types in various, sometimes, stressful and anxious circumstances. (see Appendices A, B, C, D, E, and F). Being coach of the middle school and high school swim teams also involves these same types of responsibilities that are included with the music program. The only changes are in the types of uniforms, equipment, performances, etc. (See Appendices A, B, C, D, E, and F).

Working in the CIS program has offered many administrative challenges this year because the director's position has been vacant since August, 1994. I have had to serve often as the director and teacher communicating between our school officials, the CIS Board of Directors, and the community. I have had the sole responsibility of planning all activities and trips, maintaining all CIS records of my 15 students, communicating with the teachers and parents of the CIS students, arranging appropriate rewards for achievements, reporting expenditures, and referring students with special needs (see Appendices E, F, H, and J).

As the Teacher Support Specialist for the last two school years I have served as a mentor for three new first year teachers. This has meant being an encourager and friend for the new teacher, answering questions about all areas of the school from policies to personalities, informally observing the classroom when requested, and introducing the new teacher to the faculty and staff (see Appendix B).

As an off-campus instructor for Brewton-Parker College, I have had to maintain all attendance records and grades weekly to have these sent back to the college office. Since the class is off-campus, I have also had to be sure text books were made available to the students, make special orders for the equipment to be used, and handle all my printing and copying needs for the class (see Appendix A).

ANALYSIS OF LEADERSHIP TECHNIQUES, STRATEGIES
Leadership starts with establishing people as your number one priority and being available to these people. Showing a sincere interest in and care for individuals and/or groups is and encouragement to those you lead. It is important to lead by example in areas of dependability, responsibility, honesty, and trust. Taking pride in work, fairness, consistency, goal setting, and time management are other areas in which a leader should be careful to set good examples.

A leader needs to be a strong motivator and good organizer knowing how and when to delate responsibilities to others through teacher empowerment, site-based management, and collaboration. Leaders have to lead in a way that creates a desires to follow willingly. Sometimes people feel unappreciated and unthanked as if no one really notices the work done or the effort put forth. Through the use of praise, positive recognition, notes of appreciation, special rewards, etc., a leader can continue to motivate and lead employees in greater achievement and performance.

DESCRIPTION OF LEADERSHIP PRACTICES
Through my classroom and extra curricular activities I have many opportunities to practice leadership. As a mentor for new teachers I am a leader in orienting the new faculty members to our school as well as our entire school system (see Appendix B). In my coaching position, choral director position, and assistant band director position there are many opportunities for leadership. All nine leadership competencies are handles regularly as a leader in these three areas (see Appendix E).

Working in the CIS program without a director this year has provided many situations in which I had to act as the director or leader. Rather than just staying the classroom and working with the students I have had to work with the board of directors, school administrators, teachers, parents, and community leaders. I have been responsible for all paperwork and communications that would normally be handled by the director (see Appendices E, H, and J).

ASSESSMENT OF EFFECTIVENESS

My leadership style has been effective. My decisions have not always been popular with everyone but have been proven to be effective and the best choice for those involved. I have an enjoyable and controllable classroom. My students are learning in a positive environment. The mentoring of new teachers has been a good experience in helping new teachers adjust to our school. The CIS program is doing well in spite of a lack of unity among board members and the lack of director for most of the year.

We have an excellent middle school band and choral program. I have the respect of students and parents in both the band and chorus. We also have strong parental and community support for these two programs. In addition, I have felt a great sense of pride and accomplishment in establishing, coaching, and leading the swim team at our high school and middle school. We will enter our fourth season as a team this fall.

IMPROVEMENT ACTIVITIES

The most recent workshop I attended was the GMEA (Georgia Music Educator's Association) convention held each January 1995, in Savannah. This was a three day convention and with many classes to chose from and many performances to attend. I tried to attend as many choral and keyboard events as possible. I especially enjoyed the workshops dealing with electronic keyboard labs. I hope we will eventually have an electronic keyboard lab for our sixth and seventh grade general music classes. For me, this conference provides a time for reenergizing and renewing my excitement about being a music educator. It is good to have the opportunity to be around others in the same field an compare notes and experiences.

I also went through the RESA (Regional Educational Service Agency) TSS (Teacher Support Specialist) course. This was a ten hour course and took two quarters to complete, but it was excellent training in mentoring new teachers. The course was taught by a member who is on the RESA staff. I have since worked with three new teachers in our school helping them in whatever areas they needed help or assistance. I actually received TSS certification which is formally added to my teaching certificate as an area of certification (see Appendix B).

In addition, I have attended coach's workshops and clinics. The most recent were in Albany and Gainsville. These clinics were designed to go over the rules of the GHSA (Georgia High School Association) for swimming and to help with scheduling and general coaching techniques. This was only my third year coaching so I always welcome help in this area.

This past fall I attended a Rainbow Facilitator workshop in Thomasville presented by RESA. I was trained to be a Rainbow Facilitator for our school and have worked with a small group of sixth graders weekly helping them to adjust to the death of a parent. (see Appendix K). While working on the Teacher Support Services (TSS) certification I, along with two other teachers from our school, compiled a handbook to be used by our new faculty members. It is an excellent resource for new teachers.

Also this winter, I attended a Georgia CIS (Community in Schools) Director's Consortium Meeting. This was a three day workshop in Atlanta. I met CIS teachers and directors from all over the state of Georgia, as well as CIS leaders. This workshop was very helpful in my CIS work giving me new ideas for my CIS class and helping me communicate with others involved in CIS (see Appendix J).

The classes I have taken at the university level in educational leadership, have also helped tremendously in the area of leadership as well as making me a better classroom teacher. I presented as in-depth study of our systems use of federal funds through the Chapter I program. I have written an presented a paper on different teaching models. I taught a chapter, "Non-Directive Behavior," from C. Glickman's book Supervision of Instruction: A Developmental Approach. I read and summarized numerous journal and magazine articles about various aspects of both education and leadership. As part of course requirements, I have written several short papers in the area of instructional supervision, developed a project and an extensive handbook in personnel, written many law briefs in the area of school law (see Appendices A, D, E, G, H, and I).

Each spring I teach a music education course for early childhood undergraduate majors from Brewton-Parker College's off-campus program held in Norman Park, Georgia. I developed the syllabus, criteria for grades, lecture material and activities for this class (see Appendix A). All of these activities are helping me to become stronger in my leadership capabilities.

FUTURE ADMINISTRATIVE GOALS/DIRECTIONS

My most immediate goal is to complete the NL-5 certification. I have one course left and should be able to take that class in the summer quarter. I plan to immediately begin work toward my six year degree in Administration/Supervision, possibly entering the doctoral program.

I hope to first be an assistant principle at the middle school or high school level. Then I hope to move to a principal's position. I do not think I would like to work in the central office since I really enjoy being around students and their classrooms and activities. I want to stay current in the field of leadership by reading recent publications and research, by remaining active in workshops and conferences, and by communicating with other leaders.

High School
Leadership Portfolio Narrative

Table of Contents

Teaching Responsibilities

As an English teacher for ten years, I have taught a variety of high school English courses on the full range of ability levels. My primary teaching responsibilities have been with eleventh graders enrolled in American literature courses. I have taught basic, average, college preparatory, and honors American literature classes. I have also taught remedial freshman English and advanced placement senior English. I have taught classes ranging in size from nine to thirty-five.

In addition to traditional English courses, I have also taught journalism and mass media. In journalism, I taught students the basics of newspaper reporting, layout and design. My students published school newspapers and the yearbook, both of which received several awards at state competition.

I implemented the mass media technology program at Thomas County Central High School. Students enrolled in mass media technology produce a daily television program reporting school news. The class also produces a number of videotapes each year for special programs. Videotapes produced by the mass media technology class have won district, state, and national recognition.

Courses taught include:

Honors Junior English: A survey of American authors from the colonial period to the present forms the core of the course which also emphasizes composition skills, vocabulary development, and the research paper.

Advanced Placement English: AP English exposes students to a wide selection of world literature as they prepare for the AP English exam administered by the College Board. Students may earn up to fifteen hours of college credit through AP English.

Basic Junior English: This course utilizes works by American authors to teach basic reading and comprehension skills outlined in Georgia's Quality Core Curriculum. Composition skills and library skills are also addressed.

Mass Media Technology: Students learn the basics of news reporting as they gather and report school news and conduct on-camera interviews. Students also utilize editing equipment to produce a daily television program and other special video features.

Administrative Responsibilities

In 1992, I became chairman of the English department. As department chairman, I was responsible for administering the department's budget of $12,000. I also worked with the teachers in the department and with the administration in designing the departmental master schedule each summer. To establish a degree of consistency within the department, I led a group of teachers in developing a departmental handbook which outlines an articulated reading program, the departmental writing program, and the departmental grading system. A copy of the English department handbook is included in Appendix A.

In the fall of 1994, the death of an assistant principal resulted in an unanticipated opening. I assumed this position on an interim basis in September, 1994. My responsibilities include evaluating teachers using GTEP, administering the school's disciplinary and attendance policies, and securing substitute teachers as needed. I also work with club advisors in organizing the school's extra-curricular activities. I approve club activities and fundraisers and maintain the school calendar.

Teaching and Learning Philosophy

In teaching English, I rely on a combination of techniques including lecture, discussion, cooperative learning groups, individual and group projects, and compositions (see Appendix J). No technique is appropriate for every teaching situation; therefore, it is important that one select the technique best suited to the content and the learner or learners. I place a heavy emphasis on writing as an instructional strategy since I believe in the research which shows that writing is a highly effective learning mode (see the writing across the curriculum program in Appendix A).

I organize my curriculum into instructional units. Within each unit, there are opportunities for group work as well as individual work. Believing in a high degree of accountability, I give frequent quizzes. Each unit includes several opportunities for students to write about what they are learning.

I became an English teacher because of my appreciation for good literature. I try to share my enthusiasm for the subject in the hope that my enthusiasm will spark greater student interest.

Leadership and Philosophy Practices

Administrators have two primary tasks: showing consideration for subordinates and initiating the structure needed to accomplish the organization's mission. In providing leadership for others, I try to be very well-organized and predictable. Others know what to expect from me and can anticipate what I expect from them. I try to be the hardest working member of my department because I believe leading by example is the best way to make a positive difference.

Others accept structure more readily when they understand the rationale behind it. Therefore, I try to explain what needs to be accomplished and why it is important. Incorporating the ideas of others is necessary for consensus building. I believe that leadership should be a team effort. As many people as possible should be involved in the decision-making process. Through membership on my school's leadership team, I have participated in the shared-governance process and feel that it benefits school administrators, teachers, and students.

Analysis of methods, strategies

Technology has given teachers a number of new tools to use in the instructional process. CD Rom computer research tools have revolutionized the teaching of the research paper. Over the course of the last ten years, I have tried to constantly revise my strategies and assignments to stay current with new technology. On-line computer searching capabilities that can be carried out from the English classroom have enabled students to include a wider variety of sources in their papers. Footnotes at the bottom of the page have given way to parenthetical citations, and the meticulous typing instructions have given way to the word processor. Clearly, one's strategies must be constantly evaluated and updated.

Believing that writing is an essential skill for all students, I stress the writing process in all of my classes. I encourage students to do pre-writing activities, write, revise, edit, and rewrite as many times as is necessary to produce a quality product. I make myself available after school and before school to tutor students as needed. Students have my home phone number, and I have spent countless hours tutoring students at night on the telephone. Students know that I want them to succeed, and this encourages them to work harder.

Students in my mass media production classes produce detailed storyboards for their video productions. We then film, edit, and present their work. Students take great pride in their work when they know that they have a real audience. An example storyboard is included in Appendix N.

When students are writing their formal research papers in the spring, I try to plan an informal "writing conference" with each student during the outlining stage. This gives me an opportunity to give a student advice about the direction of his or her paper before the student invests too much time writing the first draft. I use standardized evaluation forms on all major writing assignments. These forms help me be certain that I stay consistent with expectations. Since students are provided with copies of the forms in advance, they are able to see exactly how they will be evaluated. This helps reduce student anxiety.

One activity that I developed is in use in several high schools across South Georgia. It is an essay revision/analysis activity that leads student through a series of specific exercises to help them improve the quality of their writing. This activity has helped make the revision step of the writing process more meaningful for my students and students of other teachers who have adopted the activity. A copy of the activity is included in Appendix J.

Representative Course Syllabi including Assignments, Examinations, and Readings

At the beginning of each school year I issue a syllabus in each class. The syllabus includes a narrative description of the course, a list of major instructional objectives, a list of texts and other readings, an outline of the content, class rules and regulations, course requirements, and the grading system. Sample copies of my course syllabi are included in Appendix J. The syllabus helps facilitate communication between the teacher and students and between the teacher and parents. It also serves as an outline to help provide a flexible but consistent pace for the school year. When I digress from the syllabus, it is intentional and with proper notification to students.

Awards and Recognitions

Louis B. Newton Medallion of Academic Excellence
   Awarded by Mercer University upon receipt of BA degrees in English and Christianity in June, 1985. Mercer presents the Newton medal each spring quarter to the graduate who has exhibited the highest academic achievement in that year's graduating class.

Outstanding Teacher Awards presented by the Burke County Board of Education, Spring 1986, 1987, and 1988.

STAR teacher awards 1988 and 1991

Central High School and Thomas County Teacher of the Year, 1990.

Achievement earned by my students
   1987:   Coached the region champion debate team.
   1990:   Won state honors for yearbook and newspaper.
   1991:   Won state honors for yearbook and newspaper.
   1991:   Student won district level essay competition.

1992:	Won state honors for yearbook, newspaper, and television production.
1992:	Student won district level essay competition.
1993:	Won state honors for yearbook, newspaper, and television production.
1993:	Student won district level essay competition.
1994:	Won state honors for newspaper and television production.

Improvement Activities

I have constantly sought to improve the quality of my instruction and to share my successes with others. Consequently, I have attended numerous staff development programs and have conducted or helped to conduct several others.

Staff Development/Workshops Attended:

Writing is Thorough and Efficient (Project WrITE) (Staff development activity, 1985).
Data Collection Training for TPAI (Staff development, Fall, 1986).
Writing to Win (Staff development, Fall, 1988).
Test writing workshop (Staff development, Fall, 1989)
School improvement planning (Staff development, Summer 1991)
Teaching critical thinking skills (Summer 1992).
Strategies to improve achievement in English/language arts (Staff development, Summer 1992)
Diffusing Verbal Aggression (Summer 1993).
Graphics and special effects for television (Workshop, Summer 1993).

Staff Development Activities/Workshops Conducted:

"Producing Educational Videotapes," National School Boards Association Convention, Anaheim, California, March 1993
"Producing Educational Videotapes," Georgia Association of Educational Leaders Convention, Jekyll Island, July 1993
Project Wr.I.T.E. staff development, Burke County School System, Summer 1986

Future Administrative Goals/Directions

Since I was in high school, I have had the goal of becoming a high school principal. Because I believe that the principal's role as instructional leader of his or her school is foremost among his or her responsibilities, I sought extensive experience in the classroom before entering the field of administration. I have planned my career to roughly follow this plan: ten years in the classroom; ten years as an assistant principal; and ten years as the principal of a high school.

Since I am now in my tenth year as a teacher, I am ready to move to the second major step in my career plan. During the first ten years, I have served on the school leadership team, as department chair, and as a member of the school improvement team. As an assistant principal, I hope to serve under a dynamic building principal who can act as my mentor and can help prepare me for my own principalship someday.

Leadership Portfolio Evaluation Criteria

Intern _____ Date _____

University Supervisor _____ Advisor _____

Evaluator _____

On a scale of 1 to 5 (5 being high), how successfully does the work in this portfolio meet the following criteria:

1. Evidence provided on competency completion   1   2   3   4   5

2. Well-organized   1   2   3   4   5

3. Includes appropriate information on school improvement project   1   2   3   4   5

4. Includes a variety of work (forms, memos, agendas, etc)   1   2   3   4   5

5. Shows clarity of writing   1   2   3   4   5

6. Shows conciseness of writing   1   2   3   4   5

7. Uses correct grammar   1   2   3   4   5

8. Is persuasive   1   2   3   4   5

9. Uses correct spelling   1   2   3   4   5

10. Looks neat and professional   1   2   3   4   5

11. Materials are current   1   2   3   4   5

12. Supportive evidence for narrative is provided   1   2   3   4   5

Comments _____

_____

_____

_____

_____

APPENDIX J

Course Evaluation Form

Course Prefix_____ Quarter_____

Course Number/Section_____ Instructor_____

College of Education
Student Evaluation of Course/Teaching

Rating scale is one to five with the following discriptors:
- 5 = Strongly Agree
- 4 = Agree
- 3 = Uncertain
- 2 = Disagree
- 1 = Strongly Disagree
- NA = Not Applicable

COURSE ORGANIZATION AND CONTENT

1. At the beginning of this course the instructor explained what I was going to learn and why it was relevant.   5 4 3 2 1 NA

2. The procedures regarding assignments, absences, and grading were made clear by the instructor.   5 4 3 2 1 NA

3. The examinations, papers, projects, class discussions were relevant and matched the course objectives.   5 4 3 2 1 NA

4. Class activities/assignments encouraged applications of "best educational practices".   5 4 3 2 1 NA

5. The materials and assignments were helpful in my mastery of the course objectives.   5 4 3 2 1 NA

6. This course prepared me to be a better educator.   5 4 3 2 1 NA

THE INSTRUCTOR AS A ROLE MODEL

The instructor:

7. was well prepared for each class.   5 4 3 2 1 NA

8. used a variety of class activities--lecture, small groups, simulations, etc.   5 4 3 2 1 NA

9. encouraged my involvement.   5 4 3 2 1 NA

10. was available/responsive to my concerns.   5 4 3 2 1 NA

11. respected different ideas from students.   5 4 3 2 1 NA

12. graded student work fairly and promptly.   5 4 3 2 1 NA

13. provided helpful feedback.   5 4 3 2 1 NA

14. demonstrated excellent communication skills--standard English, pacing, volume, tone. etc.   5 4 3 2 1 NA

15. encouraged higher order thinking skills.   5 4 3 2 1 NA

FREE RESPONSE SECTION

The following items allow you to express your opinions about this course directly to the instructor. This information will not be shared with the instructor until after course grades have been submitted. The instructor will receive this form exactly as you submit it.

16. The part of this course I liked **most** was:

17. The part of this course I liked **least** was:

18. Suggestions or additional comments:

- -

FIELD EXPERIENCE ACTIVITIES: If you participated in a field experience in this class, please rate the following items. If you did not have a field experience, then do not rate these items.

19. Clear expectations for your field experience were established
    prior to the activities.   5 4 3 2 1 NA

20. The field experiences were appropriate to course objectives. 5 4 3 2 1 NA

21. The instructor or _____ observed some of my
    field experiences.   5 4 3 2 1 NA

22. Feedback was provided to me about my performance from:

    the instructor.   5 4 3 2 1 NA

    the school site teacher/administrator.   5 4 3 2 1 NA

    other _____.   5 4 3 2 1 NA

23. The field experience helped me practice applications
    as presented in my college class.   5 4 3 2 1 NA

24. The total amount of time for this field experience during this quarter was
    _____ hours.

Bibliography

American Association of Colleges for Teacher Education. (1988). School leadership preparation: A preface for action. Washington, DC: Author.

American Association of School Administrators. (1982). Guidelines for the preparation of school administrators. Arlington, VA: Author.

Bacharach, S. B. (Ed.). (1990). Educational reform: Making Sense of It All. Boston: Allyn and Bacon.

Bennett, K. (1993). Coaching for leadership: Moving toward site-based management. NASSP Bulletin, 77 (552), 81-91.

Bensimon, E. M. & Neumann, A. (1993). Redesigning collegiate leadership: Teams and teamwork in higher education. Baltimore: The Johns Hopkins University Press.

Board of Examiners--Reeve, R. E., Chair. (1989, November 15). Report of NCATE reaccreditation visit of Valdosta State College. Charlottesville, VA: University of Virginia.

Bridges, E. M. (1992). Problem based learning for administrators. Eugene, OR: ERIC Clearinghouse on Educational Management, University of Oregon.

Bush, G. (1991). America 2000: An education strategy. Washington, DC: U. S. Department of Education.

Campbell, R. F., Fleming, T., Newell, L. J. and Bennion, J. W. (1987). A history of thought and practice in educational administration. New York: Teachers College Press.

Chance, E. E. & Grady, M. L. (1990). Creating and implementing a vision for the school. NASSP Bulletin, 74 (529), 12-18.

Cutlip, S., Center, A., & Bloom, J. (1985). Effective public relations. Englewood Cliffs, NJ: Prentice-Hall.

Dewey, J. (1925, 1981). Experience and nature. In J. Boydston (Ed.) John Dewey: The later works, 1925-1953. Carbondale, IL: Southern Illinois Press.

Edgerton, R., Hutchings, P., & Quinlan, K. (1991). The teaching portfolio: Capturing the scholarship in teaching. Washington, D.C.: American Association for Higher Education.

Elam, S. M., Rose, L. C. & Gallup, A. M. (1994). The 26th annual Phi Delta Kappa/Gallup Poll of the public's attitudes toward the public schools. Phi Delta Kappa, 76 (1), 41-56.

Frye, B. J. (Ed.). (1994). Teaching in college. 3rd. ed. Cleveland, OH: Info-Tec.

Georgia Department of Education. (1988). Georgia teacher certification tests: Field 23: Administration and supervision. Atlanta, GA: Author.

Georgia Department of Education. (1987). Leadership performance assessment instrument, pilot draft. Atlanta, GA: Author.

Georgia Department of Education. (1984). Quality basic education act of Georgia. Atlanta, GA: Author.

Georgia Professional Standards Commission. (1993, July 1). Education personnel preparation and certification rules and procedures. Atlanta, GA: Author.

Griffiths, D. E. (1988a). Administrative theory. In N. J. Boyan (Ed.), <u>Handbook of research on educational administration,</u> pp. 27-51. New York: Longman.

Griffiths, D. E., Stout, R. T., Forsyth, P. B. (Eds.). (1988b). <u>Leaders for America's schools.</u> Berkeley, CA: McCutchan.

Hallinger, P. & Murphy, J. (1991). Developing leaders for tomorrow's schools. <u>Phi Delta Kappan, 72</u> (7), 514-520.

Hanson, E. M. (1991). <u>Educational administration and organizational behavior. 3rd ed.</u> Boston: Allyn and Bacon.

Harvey, T. & Brolet, B. (1994). <u>Building teams: Building people.</u> Lancaster, PA: Technomic.

Hoy, W. K. & Miskel, C. G. (1991). <u>Educational administration: Theory, research, practice. 4th ed.</u> New York: McGraw-Hill.

Jackson, P. (1986). How to build public relationships that motivate real support. <u>NASSP Bulletin, 70,</u> 25-31.

Kirby, P. C. & Colbert, R. (1994). Principals who empower teachers. <u>Journal of School Leadership, 4</u> (1), 39-49.

Leithwood, K. A. (1992). The move toward transformational leadership. <u>Educational Leadership, 49</u> (5), 8-12.

McKeachie, W. J. (Ed.). (1994). <u>Teaching tips: Strategies, research, and theory for college and university teachers. 9th ed.</u> Lexington, MA: D. C. Heath.

McKernan, J. R. Jr., Chair, National Education Goals Panel. (1994). <u>The national education goals report: Building a nation of learners.</u> Washington, DC: U. S. Government Printing Office.

Midgley, C. & Wood, S. (1993). Beyond site-based management: Empowering teachers to reform schools. <u>Phi Delta Kappan, 75</u> (3), 245-252.

Milstein, M. M., and Associates. (1993). <u>Changing the way we prepare educational leaders.</u> Newbury Park, CA: Corwin Press.

Morgan, P. L. (1995, August). <u>The internship: Theory to practice.</u> Paper presented at the annual conference of the National Council of Professors of Educational Administration, Williamsburg, VA.

Murphy, J. (Ed.). (1993a). <u>Preparing tomorrow's school leaders: Alternative designs.</u> University Park, PA: The University Council for Educational Administration.

Murphy, J. (1993b). Ferment in school administration. In J. Murphy (Ed.), <u>Preparing tomorrow's school leaders: Alternative designs.</u> University Park, PA: The University Council for Educational Administration.

National Association of Elementary School Principals. (1990). <u>Principals for 21st century schools.</u> Alexandria, VA: Author.

National Association of Secondary School Principals. (1985). <u>Performance-based preparation of principals.</u> Reston, VA: Author.

National Association of Secondary School Principals. (1992). <u>Developing school leaders: A call for collaboration.</u> Reston, VA: Author.

National Commission on Excellence in Education. (1993). <u>A nation at risk: The imperative for educational reform.</u> Washington, DC: U. S. Government Printing Office.

National Council for Accreditation for Teacher Education. (1995). <u>Advanced programs in educational leadership for principals, superintendents, curriculum directors, and supervisors.</u> Prepared by the National Policy Board for Educational Administration. Washington, D.C.: Author.

National Council for Accreditation of Teacher Education. (1994). Introduction to NCATE's standards. <u>NCATE refined standards.</u> Washington, DC: Author.

National Council for Accreditation of Teacher Education. (1982). <u>Standards for the accreditation of teacher education.</u> Washington, DC: Author.

National Policy Board for Educational Administration. (1993). <u>Principals for our changing schools: Knowledge and skill base.</u> Fairfax, Virginia: Author.

Norton, C. J. (letter on file, October 23, 1990). Valdosta State College master's level program in administration and supervision is administratively approved until the next on-site state review. Atlanta: Georgia Department of Education.

Peper, J. B. (1988). Clinical education for school superintendents and principals: The missing link. In D. E. Griffiths, R. T. Stout, & P. B. Forsyth (Eds.), <u>Leaders for America's schools.</u> Berkeley, CA: McCutchan.

Richards, J. J. & Fox, A. (1990). The internship--A meaningful experience for new administrators. <u>NASSP Bulletin, 74</u> (526), 26-28.

Robbins, P. (1991). <u>How to plan and implement a peer coaching program.</u> Alexandria, VA: Association for Supervision and Curriculum Development.

Sagor, R. (1992). <u>How to conduct collaborative action research.</u> Alexandria, VA: Association for Supervision and Curriculum Development.

Schlechty, P. C. (1990). <u>Schools for the 21st century.</u> San Francisco: Jossey-Bass.

Schon, D. A. (1987). <u>Educating the reflective practitioner.</u> San Francisco: Jossey-Bass.

Seldin, P. (1993). <u>Successful use of teaching porfolios.</u> Bolton, MA: Anker Publishing Company, Inc.

Toffler, A. (1980). <u>The third wave.</u> New York: William Morrow.

Tozer, S. E., Violas, P. C. and Senese, G. B. (1995). <u>School and society: Historical and contemporary perspectives, 2nd ed.</u> New York: McGraw-Hill.

University Council for Educational Administration. (1987). <u>Leaders for America's schools: The report of the National Commission on Excellence in Educational Administration.</u> Tempe, AZ: Author.

Valdosta State College. (1989). <u>A capsule description of selected factors at Valdosta State College: A key component of a proposed South Georgia regional university.</u> Valdosta, GA: Author.

Walker, P. A. & Roder, L. R. (1993). Reflections on school-based management and teacher empowerment. <u>Journal of Law and Education, 22</u> (2), 159-175.

Watkins, B. T. (1989, October 4). Denials of reaccreditation rise sharply under new teacher education policies. In <u>Chronicle of Higher Education</u>, pp. A13-A14.

Wylie, V. L. (Ed.). (1988-1989). <u>"Creating visionary leaders:" Knowledge base document.</u> Unpublished report prepared by faculty of the Department of Educational

Administration and Supervision during self-study in preparation for National Council of Accreditation of Teacher Education (NCATE) visit conducted November 12-15, 1989. Valdosta, GA: School of Education.

Wylie, V. L. & Michael, R. O. (1989, October). <u>The knowledge base in educational administration: Serving many masters.</u> Paper presented at the annual convention of The University Council for Educational Administration, Paradise Valley, AZ.

Wylie, V. L. & Michael, R. O. (1990). School reform in Georgia: Who will bell the cat? <u>GATEways to Teacher Education, 3</u> (1), 1-9.

Wylie, V. L. & Clark, E. H. (1992). Evaluation of rigor and value as a base for restructuring the administrative internship. In F. C. Wendel (Ed.), <u>Reforming Administrator Preparation Programs,</u> (pp. 57-69). University Park, PA: The University Council for Educational Administration, UCEA Monograph.

Wylie, V. L. & Clark, E. H. (1994). Personal observations of using peer coaching to improve the administrative internship. <u>Journal of School Leadership, 4</u> (5), 543-556.